MW00736798

COMMON

& SENSE

TIMING™

Copyright 2004
Global Entity Media, Inc.

COMMON SENSE & TIMING™

Letting your sixth sense guide you to business and social success

A hands-on, practical guide to the fine art of getting ahead

Michael J. Cutino

Global Entity Media, Inc.
2090 Fifth Avenue, Ronkonkoma, New York 11779
Copyright 2004

www.commonsenseandtiming.com

COMMON

SENSE
TIMING™

COMMON SENSE AND TIMING. Copyright © 2004 by
Michael J. Cutino. All rights reserved. Printed in the United
States of America. No part of this book may be used or
reproduced in any manner whatsoever without written
permission except in the case of brief quotations embodied in
critical articles or reviews. For information, address Global
Entity Media, Inc. 2090 Fifth Avenue, Ronkonkoma, NY 11779
- 631-580-7772

Library of Congress Cataloging-in-Publication Data

Cutino, Michael J.
  Common Sense and Timing: Letting your sixth sense
guide you to business and independent success / Michael J.
Cutino - 2nd ed. ISBN 0-312-93164-6

      p.   cm.
    ISBN 0-9760871-0-3
    1. Success in business.   I. Title.
  HF5386.C94   1990
  650.1 --dc20   90-9063
                                              CIP

Printed in the United States of America
First edition: November 1990, Second edition November: 2004

www.commonsenseandtiming.com

CONTENTS

www.commonsenseandtiming.com

INTRODUCTION

We're all looking for a fast, easy way to live happily ever after — peace of mind and the American dream! We all want success and we want it now. We are all looking for a shortcut, a secret, a hint — something — but it has to be easy, cheap and not too time-consuming because, Lord knows, everything else in our lives is difficult, expensive or time-consuming.

Well, I have good news for you! The way exists and it all boils down to two simple concepts — common sense and timing. Look at the people around you — the ones in the spotlight, the ones getting things done. If you ask them, you'll find that their success is achieved through common sense and by being at the right place at the right time — that is, timing.

"But that's them," you say, "not me!" Well, it can be you. No common sense? Nonsense! We're all born with common sense — it's instinctive. The trick is to use it.

"Common sense is perhaps the most equally

*divided, but surely the most underemployed
talent in the world.*"

-Christine Collange

The same applies to being at the right place at the right time. Is it just luck? Or is it that some people direct their lives so that they position themselves to be in the right place at the right time?

In this book, I will show you how to use your common sense and timing to make life's everyday problems easier to deal with, easier to solve and easier to dissolve. I will teach you how to direct your bodily senses and channel them in positive and effective ways. Applying all of your senses will give you the confidence to make the right decisions at the right time.

In other words, I will show you to tune in to your "sixth sense." We've all heard people say, "My sixth sense told me you were going to call," or "I sensed this was going to happen." In fact, you've probably felt this way yourself. So how did you know that you were going to receive a phone call or that opportunity or disaster would strike? Are you psychic? Did angels whisper in your ear? Perhaps, but I doubt it. You were just using all of your senses. This pooling of information—your sixth sense—is just plain old common sense.

This book deals with your mind, your body and how you can make the right decision at the right time. The ideas here can help you achieve independence, confidence and stability for a success-filled future. Of course, there are no guarantees in life and I certainly can't guarantee the results you'll obtain—

only that you will indeed get results. I know this to be true because these same principles have worked in my life and if I can do it, you can, too.

I didn't start out rich or famous. I grew up in Queens during the fifties. My mom was a housewife and my dad was a sanitation engineer (back then we called them garbage men). I had two younger sisters and a talent for getting into trouble. My parents were less than thrilled when the Catholic elementary school I attended suggested that a smart-aleck kid like me would be better off in public school (I was not considered "college material"). However, I was thrilled.

I loved public school! I loved the freedom and independence. I loved math and gym. I loved the extra free time I had to watch my favorite TV programs like "Superman" and "Abbott and Costello." So many of those old black and white programs centered around newspaper offices and radio broadcast studios. I was fascinated. However, I didn't want to be like Jimmy Olson or even Clark Kent. I wanted to be like Perry White, the Editor-in-Chief. I wanted to be the boss! I didn't realize it then, but I even wanted to move a step beyond Perry White. I wanted to own that "great metropolitan newspaper."

In other words, I had the authentic American Dream. I wanted to run my own business. And so that's just what I did. I put together a cardboard box and a couple of cans of Shinola and every nice day after school, I'd go down to the neighborhood bar and offer my services as a shoeshine boy. I shined about ten pairs of shoes each day for 10 cents a shine. However, I made four times that much in tips because I was efficient, aggressive and cute. The cute part probably counted for a lot back then. In fact, it still does.

In junior high school, I ran a lawn mowing service. By high school, I added a floor-polishing business, and in college (yes, I did go), I built my own hot dog concession.

After college, I worked for a number of people doing everything from janitorial work, to managing a disco, and repairing appliances. As an appliance repairman, I sold so many service contracts that my boss suggested I concentrate on sales alone. Before long, I switched jobs and began selling insurance. From there, it was a short jump to selling advertising. Since I was good at selling ads for someone else, I thought, "Why not try selling them for my own publication?"

At the age of 28, I conceived a small magazine-like handout for nightclubs and restaurants called Nightlife. Working out of my house, I pasted a dummy magazine together, selling ads at $25 a piece and printed the first issue in 1980. I was on my way to becoming a millionaire. Or was I? Within months, I was $300,000 in debt. I owed money to everyone I knew and a lot of people I didn't know. My wife was expecting our first child, the bank was foreclosing on our home and my "luxurious" executive office was a 10x10 room in the basement of a funeral home.

Now, twenty years later, I am the chief executive officer of a multimillion-dollar business that prints three successful monthly magazines and produces a weekly entertainment update shown on cable TV networks across the country. How did I do it? You guessed it—common sense and timing.

During the last twenty years, I've learned that there are only two types of people in this world—the talkers and the doers. You can tell them apart because the talkers speak in terms of "if only". "If only I were rich..." "If only I had listened..." If only I had time..." "If only..." "If only..." "If only..." Talkers will "if only" themselves till their dying day. On the other hand, the doers speak in terms of "I'm glad". "I'm glad I did...." "I'm glad I saw ...." "I'm glad I listened...." The question is which type of person would you like to be—the person who says "If only" or the person who says "I'm glad"?

For me, the choice is simple. I'm glad I started my businesses. I'm glad I wrote this book. I'm glad you picked it up. I'm glad I can help you. I'm glad you want to learn and grow and do the most you can do. Quite frankly, the world needs more people like us. I wanted to give you thinking knowledge that will help you for the rest of your life. No one can take knowledge away from you: you can keep accumulating it everyday. Always remember that before you enter a situation, take a second and just think about the possibilities. There are no such words, as "I can't." Always think positive. It takes less energy to think positive than negative. Life is a roller coaster filled with ups and downs. Most people think the downs are a set back, but in "COMMON SENSE AND TIMING" I teach you to use those "downs" as a positive source of information and knowledge.

Remember, when one door closes, ten windows open up, plus there is always the back and side doors. After you have finished reading my book, I would like for you to think about each chapter and try to relate what you have read to yourself. When you read "Common Sense and Timing" the second time, the structure and thinking knowledge will start to set in and you will develop a whole new outlook on your life. That's why I wrote this book just for you.

Now let me show you how to put your "Common Sense and Timing" to work for you. Focus on each chapter, one at a time. Let's start working on your new outlook for life and success now by reading my first chapter.

Michael J Cutino

CHAPTER 1

What is Common Sense?

*"The three great essentials to achieve anything
worthwhile are: Hard Work, Stick-to-itiveness,
and Common Sense."*
                                    Thomas Edison

"No one tests the depth of a river with both feet."
                                    Ashanti Proverb

"Don't run with Scissors!"
                                    Your Mother

*"Do what you can with what you have
where ever you are"*
                                    Anonymous

Welcome. The keys to living and enjoying a successful, productive life are close at hand—they're
closer than you think! These keys don't come from
being born with a silver spoon in your mouth. They
aren't earned just by getting an MBA from an Ivy
League school. They don't require an annual mem-
bership fee. They don't come from spending 80 hour

weeks for 20 years slaving in a Wall Street office. Nor are they available to you from an infomercial about secret real estate methods revealed monthly to you via a multi-payment plan.

You already hold the keys to success in your hand. Believe it or not, you were born with them! You just may not be aware of it.

The purpose of this book is to show you how to uncover those keys that will open some serious doors for you. You're probably going to be surprised that you hadn't thought of using them before. You might even look back and see some places where you could have used those handy keys in the past.

So let's jump right into it. The first key that you have within you is Common Sense.

COMMON SENSE

But what is common sense? Common sense means everyday sense. It isn't something that is extraordinary or only available to people with specialized knowledge. It is simply the ability to understand, and deal with, the everyday events of life.

Examples are wearing a winter coat when it's cold outside or looking both ways before crossing the street. These are things we all know to do... using our common sense!

Where did we develop our common sense? In some cases, common sense is instinctual. For instance, you automatically hold your breath before being submerged underwater. You don't think, "The particles of oxygen in water are in a form that must be converted into energy before my body can use it." You simply know that you can't breathe underwater and act accordingly.

In other cases, common sense comes from experience. If you've ever placed your hand on a hot stove, common sense prevents you from doing it again.

Common sense also comes from teaching. Your parents and teachers probably told you to look both ways before crossing the street. In fact, they probably told you this so often that you automatically look both ways before crossing the street as an adult.

Finally, common sense comes from observation. Over your lifetime, you start to notice certain patterns and adjust your actions accordingly. For instance, you've learned that the winter isn't the best time to plan an outdoor picnic and that the summer isn't the best time to plan a ski trip.

Our common sense is adaptable, as demonstrated in the following quote:

"We should be careful to get out of an experience only the wisdom [Common Sense] that is in it — and stop there; lest we be like the cat that sits down on a hot stove-lid. She will never sit down on a hot stove-lid again — and that is well; but also she will never sit down on a cold one anymore."

Mark Twain

The difference between the cat and us is that we can use our intelligence to adapt our experience and observational common sense and broaden our abilities even further.

On a daily basis, whether we consciously think about it or not, common sense keeps us alive. It tells us how to obtain food and shelter. It tells us how to avoid injury. We all use common sense to do just that.

15

However, common sense can do even more for us. It can help us to not only survive, but to thrive. By using common sense in our businesses, financial affairs and even relationships, we can achieve not-so-common success.

This may be contrary to what you've been taught about success. Many people believe that success requires specialized knowledge and requires a college degree, graduate degree or some specialized training. While these things are all helpful, they aren't necessary for success.

For instance, the people on the following list are all people who never graduated from college, yet they achieved tremendous success.

Mark Twain
Henry Ford
Thomas Edison
Harry S. Truman
William Faulkner
Dave Thomas (Wendy's)
Bill Gates
Steve Jobs (founder of Apple)
Lawrence Ellison (Oracle Computer)
Michael Dell
David Geffen
H. Wayne Huizenga (Blockbuster Video)
Ted Turner
Ron Popeil

By no means is this a list of successful "dropouts." There are successful people in every city and state who have used common sense to make their dreams come true. We sometimes refer to these people as being "street smart." This term is opposed to "book smarts," which we use for formally educated people. However, even the most educated people need to use common sense in order to succeed.

Dr. Hugh Mann, the founder of organicMD.org, provides a great example of the need for common sense in medicine.

While doing morning rounds, Dr. Mann and his colleagues visited a patient who had a black tongue. The intern assigned to the patient had researched various diseases that caused black tongues and began to lecture the physicians in attendance on the various causes of the condition. However, one doctor interrupted the intern and asked the patient if he used black cough drops. The patient smiled, opened the drawer of his night table, and took out a package of black cough drops. The intern's face turned red as the other physicians laughed. He had failed to use his common sense to consider the obvious. Without one doctor's common sense, this patient could have undergone unnecessary procedures.

In the same way, I believe that many people are undergoing unnecessary procedures in their own lives because of the failure to use common sense in dealing with problems. So many of us spend so many years acquiring specialized knowledge and training that we forget the obvious, common sense solutions to life's challenges.

So if common sense is really the key, then why are not more people successful?

That's a good question. Maybe it's because common sense is so underrated, or taken for granted. After all, who wants to be an exciting success by just

17

being "common"? Who wants to attribute their success to something that everyone else has? Or something that's free? It doesn't make for the usual "Hollywood" type success story. And since common sense isn't very exciting, it doesn't really sell. So most people overlook their common strengths. As a result, their growth or movement toward success can become stunted.

IGNORING YOUR COMMON SENSE

In many ways, many of us are like the Persian farmer chronicled in the famous story of the "Acres of Diamonds."

There once lived an ancient Persian by the name of Al Hafed. Al Hafed owned a very large farm with orchards, grain fields and gardens. He was a content and wealthy man.

One day, a Buddhist priest visited Al Hafed. The priest sat down by the fire and told Al Hafed how the world was made. In the process, the priest explained the creation of diamonds and their worth. According to the old priest, just a handful of diamonds could purchase a whole country, and a mine of diamonds could place one's children upon thrones through the influence of their great wealth.

Al Hafed heard all of this and that night, went to bed a poor man. He was poor not because he had lost anything, but rather because he was discontented with what he had. He thought to himself, "I want a mine of diamonds!" The next morning, he sought out the priest and asked, "Will you tell me where I can find diamonds?"

The priest said, "Diamonds? What do you want

with diamonds?"

"I want to be immensely rich," said Al Hafed, "but I don't know where to go."

"Well," said the priest, "if you will find a river that runs over white sand between high mountains, in those sands you will always see diamonds."

Al Hafed said, "I will go."

Soon after, he sold his farm, collected his money, left his family in the charge of a neighbor, and set out in search of diamonds. He traveled through all of Persia, Palestine and even Europe without finding any diamonds. Finally, when his money was all spent and he was in rags, wretchedness and poverty, he stood on the shore of a bay in Barcelona, Spain. When the tide came rolling in, Al Hafed could not resist the overwhelming urge to throw himself into the incoming tide, and as a result he quickly drowned between the Pillars of Hercules.

If that were the whole of the story, it would be bad enough. However, the man who bought Al Hafed's farm was out in the garden one day when he caught a curious flash of light from the sands of the shallow stream. He reached in and pulled out a black stone having an eye of light that reflected all the colors of the rainbow. Not knowing what to make of it, he took the strange looking pebble into his house and placed it on the mantel.

A few days later, the same old priest who told Al Hafed how diamonds were made stopped by for a visit. When he saw that flash of light from the mantel, he yelled, "Here is a diamond—here is a diamond! Has Al Hafed returned?"

"No, no; Al Hafed has not returned and that is not

a diamond; that is nothing but a stone; we found it right out here in our garden," said the farmer.

"But I know a diamond when I see it," said the old priest; "that is a diamond!"

Together, they rushed to the garden and found other diamonds even more beautiful, and more valuable. In the end, this farm became the site of the diamond mines of Golconda, which is said to have produced the most magnificent diamond mines in history.

Al Hafed, having thrown away his current wealth and contentment, had literally walked away from acres of diamonds in pursuit of a fortune in the unknown.

This story was initially told by Russell H. Conwell. In 1870, he heard this story while riding in a camel caravan along the valley between the Tigris and Euphrates Rivers in Mesopotamia. To the other tourists in the caravan, this was just another alluring story, but to Conwell, it illustrated a great truth—the riches we seek are often in our own back yards, if we will just take the time to dig for them there.

Conwell returned to America to find his own acre of diamonds. He served as the pastor to a Baptist church in Pennsylvania for 43 years. During that time, he gave numerous lectures, wrote 40 books and eventually founded Temple University. During his lectures, he often spoke of Al Hafed and his lost acres of diamonds.

Many people today could stand to hear that lecture. They are like Al Hafed. They are already rich; perhaps not in land or money, but in common sense. Yet, they sell their common sense short in pursuit of mantras, yoga, acupuncture, meditation, instant wealth, infomercials, and a hundred other "mind expanding" techniques when the truth of the matter is that they already possess everything they will ever need—their common sense. Therefore, while they are busy trying the latest 12-step program, deep breathing regimen, or real estate scam, others are enjoying success, happiness and abundance.

RECOGNIZING YOUR OWN COMMON SENSE

One of the things that's so important to utilizing your common sense is to recognize instances where you are using it and those instances when you are not using it. Since common sense does seem so common and so obvious, it can often be difficult to see.

Take a look back at things you've done in the last week. Which ones demonstrate you were using your common sense? Simple examples of common sense: filing your taxes on time, driving slower in the rain, spending time with your kids, spending extra time on a difficult task and submitting an idea for a new product at work.

Still taking that look back at last week, which things were examples of not using common sense? Yes, you need to be able to identify these moments if you want to grow and prevent these things from recurring. Simple examples of not using common sense: Believing in someone who has established a record of lying to you, knowing that you need to study for that college exam, but avoiding it instead to watch TV, investing in that bridge in New York, etc. So take a good straight look at these weak spots. Recognize them. Make yourself aware. Don't keep repeating your mistakes.

If you didn't do anything last week where you used your common sense or even didn't use your common sense, and you didn't have any successes or mistakes or failures, then you need to get off your butt and start participating in life!

In this book, I will show you how to use your common sense to attain anything you will ever want from life. I have done it and so have thousands of other people. Why not you?

SUMMARY

Common Sense

You have common sense already. It is developed from the following: instinct (e.g., holding your breath underwater); experience (e.g., not touching a hot stove); teaching (e.g., being told by your mother to look both ways before crossing the street); and observation (e.g., no skiing in the summer time).

We can apply our common sense not just to survival, but also to our business, financial affairs, and our relationships—there are an infinite number of ways to use our common sense (unlike the cat in Twain's quote regarding the hot stove—be grateful we're not cats with only a limited type of common sense).

Ignoring Your Own Common Sense

Don't be like the story of Al Hafed; wasting time and energy looking all over the place for something you already have within you.

Recognizing Your Common Sense

Learn to recognize your common sense in action. It's pretty obvious, and therefore not always easy to recognize. Learn to recognize these actions in which you would normally ignore your own common sense. An impulse action is the result of not using your common sense. What do you do when someone tries to punch you? You move out of the way. That is an impulsive reaction. You are giving a speech and you are asked a question, what do you do? "You think before you speak", you mentally find the right answer. This is a great example to using your common sense in your every day life.

ACTION ITEMS:

1.   Are you in touch with your common sense? Take a look at the things you've been up to lately. Have you been looking for a job, but you haven't even cracked open the newspaper to look at what's out there? Have you been meaning to re-organize your desk at work, but you spend you're time changing the screensaver on your computer? Did you buy something you wanted really badly, only to find that it doesn't work like you expected?

Make a list of the things that you've done lately that show maybe a little slippage in your common sense. Don't beat yourself up over these things, just recognize them for what they are.

On your list next to each of these issues, write what you could have done or could do, using your common sense, to get them resolved or prevent them from occurring again in the future.

This will help you recognize where your common sense is not kicking in and will improve your awareness of the weak spots. It will also demonstrate to you that you do have within you the common sense and power to take a better approach on all future actions and decisions of your life. This should prove to be empowering.

2.   **Identifying good common sense.** Make a list of the things that you have done lately that are good examples of common sense. These may be so obvious that they're hard to identify. But list them any way. Get used to seeing them. Examples are preparing in advance for a speech, meeting your child's teacher to discuss the status of his/her education, taking your car in for scheduled maintenance, etc.

Exciting? No. Common sense? Absolutely.

CHAPTER 2

Timing Counts

"Success is more a function of consistent common sense than it is of genius."
                                                        An Wang

"It is circumstances and proper timing that give an action its character and make it either good or bad."
                                                        Agesilaus (444-360 B.C.)

"Observe due measure, for right timing is in all things the most important factor."
                                                        Hesiod (ca. 800 B.C.)

"Timing is everything."
                                        Somebody with Common Sense

Animals have an instinctive sense of timing. Birds know when to build a nest, when to fly south, when to fly north. Bears know when to hibernate. Salmon rely on an instinctive sense of timing to know when to swim upstream to spawn.

Perhaps it is just a biological imperative, but animals have an innate sense of timing and harmony that guides their lives. As humans, we have the same kinds of instincts. We know when it's time to eat. We take shelter when it's too cold or too hot. We rely on our senses to nurture and protect our bodies.

However, all too often, we don't continue that instinctive reliance when it comes to our careers or projects. We spend our time weighing pros and cons, looking at all the angles, imagining all the outcomes of any given action. We think too much! We are so busy debating possibilities that we often act too late.

Timing is a combination of instinct and intellect. When we toss all the combinations around, when we try to narrow the odds (whatever they might be), we're practicing. We're fine-tuning. This can be good. The problem arises when we never make the leap from preparation to performance. It's fine to consider all the outcomes that may develop from any major action we could take, but the bottom line is our knowing when to make our move — and then making it.

> *"A great man always considers the timing before he acts."*
>
> Chinese Proverb

PRACTICE MAKES PERFECT

Athletes have a strong sense of timing. They develop it through practice. A boxer doesn't knock out his opponent because he gets lucky. He K.O.'s his rival because he sees the opportunity for an open shot and his "instinctive" (that is, trained) sense of timing acts on it. Bam!

When you see it, you've got to go for it. There may

not be a second chance. You've watched Olympic skaters. Every move is coordinated, every jump is planned. This is split-second timing. But they don't just put on their skates and win the gold. What you're seeing is the finished product after thousands of hours of planning and practice. Look at gymnasts. They know where their bodies are. Again, it's planning and timing.

Where would trapeze artists be without timing? Or airline pilots? Or your local pizza parlor? Imagine calling the pizzeria and ordering a pie with everything on it. You ask when it will be ready. The pizza man says he doesn't know. Doesn't he have a clock? Is he out of mozzarella? Is the oven broken? Is he backed up with forty orders? That is no way to run a business!

The problem with this pizza man is lack of planning and practice. To be successful, you have to have some idea of how long it will take to produce the finished product, whether you are making a pizza, repairing a car, or publishing a book. It is very important to set a goal for yourself and a time limit to achieve that goal. Sometimes you'll misjudge the amount of time involved, but you can't leave a situation open-ended. You want to know when! And everyone you deal with wants to know when also.

Examine all the parts of what it is you want to do. Determine what ingredients you need. Determine how long it takes to order supplies. Get to know every aspect of what it is you want to do. Know every part, every ingredient, from the smallest details all the way up to the big picture. And practice all the actions necessary. If it's not feasible to physically practice it, mentally practice it. The timing will then come naturally, just like it does for an athlete.

Plan Tomorrow Today

Planning and organizing means knowing the big "when"—when timing for your goal becomes critical for action. There is no way you can gain a sense of timing without getting yourself organized. You have to know where everything is, how to get information you don't have, who to ask, and what comes next. Start by making lists. Write everything down. Categorize it. Classify it. File it into memory.

Everyone is a walking library of information. Organized people know how to retrieve and use that knowledge. They know how much time is available to them and how they're going to use it. They can estimate how much time is involved in any project they can undertake. This comes from planning and plain old common sense.

Do you know what you're going to be doing tomorrow? Do you have a calendar or appointment book? Take a look at it. How much do you have scheduled? What will you be doing at eleven o'clock? If you don't know, take ten minutes now and plan your day. Write down something for every hour.

Don't just think about it. Don't just say, "Well, I'm going to the office, and then maybe I'll stop by the cleaners on my lunch hour, or I'll call Susie if I have a minute." Write down exactly what you intend to accomplish tomorrow.

Write down what you're doing at work, what errands have to be done, and what time your going to do them. Make yourself a schedule for one day, and then (this is the hard part) follow it! Do everything your list says to do. And cross off items as you complete them.

At the end of the day, review your list. Did you get everything done? Did you misjudge your time? Carry over the things undone to the next day and make a new list. The key is to plan, plan, plan.

Schedule Some Daydream Time

When you make this detailed plan, throw in some daydream time. For instance, at 3 o'clock, you're going to sit quietly and let your mind wander where it will. Plan to take fifteen minutes on your lunch hour just to sit in the park and look at people. You have to give yourself leisure time. But you need to plan for it. Build the time into your schedule; otherwise your life is a series of unplanned days with some scheduled hours thrown in.

I know, organization does not come easily to some people, but there is no way you're going to get ahead and reach that goal without making a plan. There is no way the pizza man will succeed if he doesn't know where he stored the cheese, if he doesn't have a recipe, and if he can't produce the pie on time.

What's true for the pizza man is true for you. You have to set your goal and plan how to get there. When you've made your lists and thought out several angles, you'll recognize when an opportunity arises that fits your possibilities, and you'll act on it. That's what timing is all about.

"No" Means "Not At This Time"

Never be afraid of failure. If you think you've failed, reevaluate the problem to see if you can find another solution. How else can you approach it? Salespeople are often faced with rejection. For every client that says yes, eight or ten say "no." The key for a salesperson is to learn not to take "no" personally. After all, just because Miss Scarlett said "no" on Tuesday doesn't mean she'll say "no" on Friday.

Circumstances change. Timing changes.

Suppose you want to sell your car. You do your homework and you know it's worth $6,000. You put an ad in the paper, and the next day someone offers you $5,500. You probably say "no." You think you can get $6,000 (never mind that the 8-Track player no longer works — it's an antique!).

A month and a few low offers later, you still haven't sold your car. Payments are starting on the new car. Winter's coming. Someone again offers you $5,500. This time you probably say "yes." Why?

Circumstances change. Timing changes.

You've weighed the odds of getting $6,000 and re-evaluated your position. Most often a "no" in business means "not at this time" as opposed to "not ever."

FOLLOW-UP

Remember, you have nothing to lose if someone says "no" and everything to gain if they say "yes."

So what if Professor Plum says he won't order a dozen Marvelous Murdering Mousetraps today. You didn't lose the sale. You just haven't made it yet. If he ordered the mousetraps and then cancelled the order, you'd have lost the sale — maybe.

So next week, you call the professor again to see if he could use the mousetraps. And when he says "no," you send him more literature on why they are the best mousetraps ever made. And you call him again the next week.

By now, you're either on a first-name basis or he's told you to get lost. But if you've been friendly, polite and helpful, he won't be rude to you. He'll tell you "no," but if he ever needs a mousetrap he'll call you. Put a star next to his name in the organized list of possibilities you have made. You don't have to call him every week, but stay in touch with him.

This is called "follow-up"—a critical part for understanding Timing and making it work for you. You did not take the original "no" for an answer. But if you ever expect to sell this man a mousetrap, you must stay in touch with him. Put him on your mailing list. Every three weeks, send him mousetrap memos. Someday, this man will need a mousetrap or his friend will, and that's when he'll call you. But only if you've keep in contact. Otherwise, he'll go right to the Yellow Pages and forget all about you.

Follow-up is just as important when you get a "yes" as when you get a "no." If you're organized and you're following up, your timing will improve. Before you know it you're going to collect a lot of "yeses."

For instance, let's say Professor Plum bought ten mousetraps. Terrific! You made a nice commission. Thanks Professor! Now what?

You call him next week to thank him for the order. How are the mousetraps working out? Need any more? And a few weeks after that, you call again. Does he have any friends who need mousetraps? You put him on your mailing list and continue to send mousetrap memos.

A satisfied customer will tell his friends about you.

Word of mouth can spread far and wide; it is the world's most effective advertising. And it doesn't cost you a cent. See, you're making money already!

Selling Your Self

Sometimes follow-up means taking a few mouse-traps back. It means soothing upset clients and offering alternative solutions. If Mrs. Peacock can't stand the sight of those dead mice, tell her straight out that your product is not for her. Use your common sense. She obviously needs a cat.

Then help her get one! Because what you are selling is not really mousetraps; what you're selling is yourself. And when Mrs. Peacock tells her garden club what a nice, helpful person you are, you'll get several orders for mousetraps (or cats).

I want to emphasize the significance of selling yourself. Everything we've been working toward so far has to do with the packaging and marketing of you and your ideas—from what you wear, to how you speak, who you know and how you're going to find the people you need to know.

You are organizing yourself. You are promoting yourself.

And the reason you are doing all of this is because you want something that you don't have now. Don't lose sight of that goal. What you are working toward is a new you—a more experienced you, a better you, a wealthier you. Keep visualizing whatever it is you want to accomplish. Remember, you're going to get there by using your common sense and better utilizing the timing of situations. You're planning, you're organizing, and you're using every day to get closer to your dream.

"Common sense tells us that the things of the earth exist only a little, and that true reality is only in dreams."
Charles Baudelaire (1821–1867), French poet, critic.

LOOK FOR OPPORTUNITIES AND TAKE ACTION

I want to share a story with you I know you will enjoy. Once you start to understand the theory behind Common Sense and Timing, you will start to play with it, learning to recognize opportunities and using it to take action and thereby increasing your success and your ability to advance yourself.

I'm the publisher of an entertainment magazine, New York Nightlife. I was under-capitalized from the very start. I had only $4,500. Today, it takes at least $5 million to launch a magazine—and there is no guarantee that it will succeed.

After two years of trying to wheel and deal, I had to do something to get the exposure necessary so people would become aware of my publication and buy it on the newsstand. I couldn't afford advertising on any radio station, let alone any of New York's top ten. I had to figure out how to get free radio advertising and, what's more, have it timed for when over-the-counter magazine sales were slow and when the advertising agencies were planning their next advertising budgets.

It seemed impossible. But nothing is impossible if you use your common sense and try to look at all the angles. Remember planning, organizing, looking for opportunities and knowing the right time to pounce!

Everyone likes good press and favorable publicity. Radio personalities are no different; at least that's what I was hoping!

I did some research to find out who was the hottest disc jockey in New York. Then I contacted his radio station and told them I was going to do a cover story on them with a picture of their terrific DJ on the cover.

When the disc jockey heard about this, he was thrilled. The station management was so ecstatic about the free publicity that they gave me carte blanche!

When my magazine came out, everyone was happy—especially the DJ, who announced all week long on the air that he was on the cover of Nightlife. He talked up my magazine so much that he continued getting phone calls about it for two weeks.

There was no way I could put a price tag on the amount of free radio publicity I received. My total newsstand sales doubled! Advertising agencies heard and called to place advertising. And then I started receiving calls from other radio stations asking me to give the same exposure to their DJs!

I started trading radio time for advertising in my magazine. Not only was this a positive move for my business, it was a good move for the radio stations. An awareness of Nightlife was broadcast to over 8 million listeners! I never could have afforded it! My $4,500 magazine is now valued at over $6 million, and I've expanded to three other publications and two local TV shows.

Another point to remember from my experience is that you can do something good for yourself that also benefits others—creating a win-win situation. You don't have to reveal all your reasons for your move. If you make the first move, your "target" will be so flattered that he'll respond exactly as you want him to.

It's like playing tic-tac-toe. The guy who goes first always has control of the game. If you can master tic-tac-toe, you're on your way! But unlike tic-tac-toe, you can create a win-win situation—where everyone wins!

So whatever your goal may be, get out there and look for opportunities, make the opportunities happen, and when the timing is right, take action!

A Life Examined—Walt Disney

When Disney went off to Hollywood after his film company went bankrupt in Kansas, he made the rounds of the studios. He was hoping to get a job as a director (he always thought big), but there were no jobs available. He was finally hired as an extra in a cavalry scene.

This was not the way to make it in Hollywood! Disney realized that the only way he was going to get anywhere was with his cartoons. He fired off an impressive and self-confident letter to a previously encouraging New York film distributor, citing his relocation to the West Coast and enclosing a preview of the Alice film. In response, he received a telegram offering him a six-cartoon deal at $1,500.00 apiece.

Now that he had a commitment from New York, Walt was able to ask his brother, Roy, for backing, and together they formed Disney Brothers Studios. Disney contacted his old buddy, Ub Iwerks, and Ub came to Hollywood to work for Disney's new company.

The short films kept improving in quality and getting more expensive to produce. Disney always seemed to need just a little bit more money, but his work was beginning to be noticed favorably, and he was gathering a following. He signed another contract to produce 18 more films in the Alice series at $1,800 per film, and the group moved to a new studio. With that move, they changed the name to Walt Disney Studios.

After two years of doing Alice films, it was time to move on to something else. Disney was getting bored. The founder of Universal Pictures suggested to the distributor that he'd like to see a cartoon series about a rabbit. Oswald the Lucky Rabbit became Disney's first all-animated cartoon.

When the original contract was up, Disney was confident that he could ask for $2,500.00 a cartoon. However, the distributor had been working behind his back and had approached all of Disney's Oswald cartoonists. The deal would be $1,800.00 a cartoon or the staff would leave Disney's studio and create Oswald elsewhere.

Since Universal owned Oswald and Disney didn't, Walt found himself backed into a corner. He couldn't afford to make the cartoons at such a low price. On the other hand, Oswald was his major income-producer.

Disney was never one to give up. He decided to cut his losses and start again. The majority of the staff left, with the notable exception of Iwerks. Disney had learned that it was important to retain control of your creations.

Together, he and Ub began collaborating on a new cartoon series about a mouse—a mouse they named

Mortimer.

It was 1927 and the beginning of the "talkies." Disney was excited about the possibilities of adding sound to his animations. He went off to New York to gather information on how to put together a soundtrack. He found that many companies were making records to accompany the films. But there seemed to be too many problems associated with this practice. Disney wanted a way to add sound to the film itself; otherwise everything might get out of sync.

He intuitively understood that now was the time to focus on sound. Talkies were going to be big business, and he wanted to be part of it. However, his first venture working with an orchestra and sound effects people was a disappointment. He'd invested over a $1,000 to add sound to his mouse cartoon, and the music people didn't seem to understand how to pace the sound with the animations on the screen.

Disney decided to direct the next recording session himself. He told everyone what to do and when to do it, and he personally did the cartoon voices.

The results were what he hoped for, and he'd learned another valuable lesson: sometimes you have to do it yourself.

Now he just had to sell it. He showed his talking cartoon to several major distributors, but they were not enthusiastic. Disney couldn't understand it. He knew he had a winner.

A Public relations man who was running a movie house on Broadway explained to Disney that the only way to sell the series was to create public demand for it. To do that, he'd have to release it privately. The publicist, Harry Reichenbach, offered

Disney five hundred dollars a week for a two-week run of the first cartoon with sound, "Steamboat Willie," starring Mickey Mouse (Disney's wife had disliked the name Mortimer—another valuable Common Sense rule to remember—listen to your spouse!). Disney needed the money (as always) and accepted.

It was the right move at the right time.

Disney's creative triumph was heralded from Variety to The New York Times. Film distributors began calling. But Disney had learned his lesson with the Oswald fiasco. Mickey Mouse was his, and he wasn't selling the rights to anyone.

He eventually made an agreement for distribution with his sound company, Cinephone.

As the mouse took off, Disney kept creating and trying new ideas. He began working on animations to classical music and developed The Skeleton Dance, set to Grieg's "March of the Dwarfs." It didn't go over right away. With most new ideas, people initially reject the unfamiliar. But self-confident creators are persistent, and rejection does not get in their way. It was only a matter of time before Disney's "Silly Symphonies" were accepted and between them and Mickey Mouse, he was becoming famous.

A Life Examined—Milton Hershey

Not unlike Disney, who ventured to Hollywood, Milton Hershey decided it was time to establish himself in New York. With yet another loan from his Aunt Mattie, and the unfailing support of his mother, Milton went to work for a candy maker by day and cooked his own confections in his landlady's kitchen at night. It wasn't long before he had a following and enough money to open Hershey's Fine Candies on Sixth Avenue. Ever loyal, his mother and aunt came to help him. It was like old times in Philadelphia.

But the more successful he became, and the bigger his sales, the larger his debts grew. He constantly needed money for sugar, and his family kept loaning it to him. After three years of making a successful product that somehow kept losing money, Hershey had to close his doors again. By this time, he owed several thousand dollars, he was being evicted from both his apartment and his shop, and his equipment was about to be repossessed.

With his last dollars, Hershey managed to get some of his cookware to the railroad station, where he shipped it collect to himself in Pennsylvania and then bought a one-way ticket home. Since he had no money left, he ate what remained of his candy for dinner.

Hershey arrived back in his hometown (the future Hershey, Pennsylvania) on a cold and rainy night. His mother's house was too far away to walk to, and he had no money. The next day, his cooking equipment would arrive at the station, and he had no idea how he was going to pay for it. He wasn't even thirty years old and already he'd managed to fail at the same business in Philadelphia, Chicago, New Orleans, and New York. By this time, most people would have given up, but persistence is crucial.

For every door that closes, another one opens. Hershey had come home hoping to start again somehow. And as fate would have it, he ran into his old friend, Lebbie, from the Philadelphia days. Lebbie took Hershey in, fed him supper, ran him a hot bath, gave him dry clothes, and sent him to bed. Exhausted, Milton fell asleep. When he awoke the next morning, Lebbie had already retrieved the cookware, rented shop space, and was ready to invest his life savings to set up another candy making business with Hershey. It was this one that finally worked.

Now you may be saying that's all well and good for Hershey and Disney because even though they went bankrupt repeatedly, they always managed to find some money to get them started again. But what about me? I don't have Aunt Mattie, or a Lebbie, or a brother Roy. My whole family thinks I'm nuts and they wouldn't loan me a nickel...

If that's the case, then you have to find other sources. You go to friends, you go to strangers. You swap, you barter, you trade. And you persist. Being at the right place at the right time helps, but first you have to make it to the right time, then you have to make it to the right place. Common sense is the ability to know what to do at the right time. Timing is not just a matter of circumstance. It is a matter of persistence.

When you've practiced, planned, organized, followed-up, dreamed, stayed positive, collected your "nos", not given up, kept an eye out for opportunities and taken action by pouncing at the right time — that's Timing. And that will mean success for you!

Do you really think Hershey and Disney succeeded only by being bailed out by their family and friends?

"From now on, I think it is safe to predict, neither the Democratic nor the Republican Party will ever nominate for President a candidate without good looks, stage presence, theatrical delivery, and a sense of timing."

James Thurber (1894–1961), U.S. humorist, illustrator After the Kennedy-Nixon debates

SUMMARY

Timing does count. But a sense of timing only works when you've surrounded yourself with all parts of your goal. Your goals need to be comprised by the following:

Practice

Know your goals backwards and forwards, just as athletes practice their moves until they can perform smoothly without needing to consciously think about every move.

Plan and Organize

Do you know what you're going to do tomorrow? Organized people know how much time is available to them and how they're going to use it. They can estimate how much time is involved in any project they can undertake. Get out that agenda or appointment book for tomorrow and jot down a task for each hour plan your day it can be as simple as a list. Whatever you don't complete, move it to the next day. And don't forget to schedule some daydream time!

"No" Means "Not At This Time"

Not every one at bat will end up with a hit , and sometimes a hit results in an out, too. Not every sales call is going to result in a sale. Not every effort will succeed (remember Hershey and Disney's bankruptcies). However, most often a "no" in business means "not at this time" as opposed to "not ever."

Follow-Up

A "no" now, may result in a "yes" later. Follow-up with each person you contact. Establish yourself with them. Become a known, reliable entity to them. Make sure they're happy with your service or product. A satisfied customer or contact may recommend you to someone else. Wait for the opportunity. It's all in the timing.

Sell Your Self

Everything we've been working toward has to do with the packaging and marketing of you and your ideas— from what you wear, to how you speak, and to who you know and how you're going to find the people you need to know.

Visualize whatever it is you want to accomplish. Organize yourself. Promote yourself. Sell yourself.

Look For Opportunities and Make It Happen

Remember, what you dream can come true. So dream big! Someone long ago dreamed of flight, cell phones, and the Internet. What are you dreaming about? A house? A career? Wealth? Dream it, understand it, and look for opportunities to make it happen! Take action!

Look for it. Make it happen. I would never have gotten where I am today if I had thrown my hands up in the air at the first sign of difficulty. Practice, Plan and Organize, Collect your No's, Follow-Up, Sell Your Self, Dream Big, and Go For It! Success is just beyond your next "No!"

ACTION ITEMS

To help you integrate these skills into your day-to-day existence, here are a few action items you can do:

1. Buy yourself an appointment book, scheduler, day-timer, PDA, or just a simple calendar or checklist. At the end of each day, plan each hour of the next day. In the morning of each day, review the things you have planned to do. Anything not completed by the end of the day should be moved to the next day. Don't forget to plan some daydream time!

2. Think about your goals. Jot down a list of every aspect of your goal. If it's a house you want, write down where you want to live, how many rooms does it need to have, how big a yard, how close to the city or how far into the country. Review this list on a monthly basis. Revise it as needed. Make sure you know your goal. Know it. Know all the parts of it. Dream about it.

3. Follow-up on your goals, your commitments, your contacts. Make a list of your goals, commitments, and contacts (PDA's or schedulers are good for keeping this info handy — see #1). Don't let those opportunities turn a "no" into a "yes" slip by!

4. Stephen King's first few books were rejected by publishers many times. Keep a notebook of your "rejections" and figure out what you can learn from them. Can you turn any of them around? When you get a "yes" treat yourself to something special. Write down what you learned from your "yes" — you may want to revisit this occasionally when you get more

than one "no."

5.   Read biographies of famous people who have accomplished great things. This will allow you to familiarize yourself with the ups-and-downs they have faced and also see how they took advantage of opportunities and took action. Were those people really different than you? Don't know whom to choose? Read about someone in the same industry as your interest. Read about someone who's not in the same industry. Find out what obstacles they faced and how they got around them. You don't have to buy any books–shelves full of wonderful biographies await you at your local public library free of charge.

Here are some suggestions:

Martin Luther King
Lance Armstrong
Edmund Hillary
Oprah Winfrey
Chuck Yeager
Peggy Fleming
Mother Theresa
Gandhi
Tiger Woods
Madonna (either one)
Military Figures
Presidents
Film Actors/Actresses

CHAPTER 3
How to Focus

"Most people have no idea of the giant capacity we can immediately command when we focus all of our resources on mastering a single area of our lives."
Anthony Robbins

"The successful man is the average man, focused."
Unknown

An important element of Common Sense and Timing is how well we are able to focus. The ability to focus on goals, problems, and people is a critical skill that anyone yearning for success must master. If we are unable to focus, productivity is impossible.

"If you chase two rabbits, both will escape."
Chinese Proverb

As you shall see, there are many aspects of focus that should be understood, and with a good sense of self-discipline, using and improving your focus skills can help you through many work, family, and social situations.

WHEN TO FOCUS

We use our five senses every day to make decisions and to accomplish what we want to achieve. Some things we do automatically. We wake up, get out of bed, go into the bathroom, brush our teeth. We don't focus on or think about these things. We automatically make our coffee and fix breakfast. We probably make a similar breakfast every working day because we have a routine and we function without considering alternatives.

Okay, if we're not focusing, we're in a rut. But if we ate breakfast in a different place every day — if we ate at the diner instead of at home, or if we ate at home instead of McDonald's — we'd have to think about choices. On a daily basis, we'd be overwhelmed with the constant thinking about silly, less important choices like "Should I order the Quarter Pounder or should I order the Big Mac instead?" Everyday, we could order or make something different. We'd probably stick with it for a day or two. But eventually, we'd fall into a new routine and stop focusing once again.

Watch out. You may be in a "habit," which according to Webster is "a state of body, natural or acquired; mode of growth; aptitude acquired by practice, custom, manner."

I strongly recommend that you analyze your positive and negative habits. A change is always good for the mind and body, and it could put you into a new frame of mind. For example, maybe you're getting up at nine o'clock and starting your workday at ten. If you change your nine o'clock wakeup habit to seven o'clock, this would give you more productivity and an added start for the day. It is very important to consider and use all the resources possible to become successful. Why not? They are there for the taking!

Some things we have to do on automatic pilot. Not thinking about breakfast frees our mind for more important ideas. But, and this is most critical — sometimes our whole life is on automatic pilot! We're in a comfortable (or maybe uncomfortable) rut and going nowhere. How do we change?

Sometimes it seems too overwhelming. You just don't know where to start and you don't have the energy. That's probably why you picked up this book. You're not quite satisfied with where you are now and you're looking for a quick and easy way to feel a little better.

Well, you've already taken the first step. By picking up this book, you are beginning to focus on the fact that you don't have everything exactly as you would like it.

VISUALIZING

Your next step is to recognize what's worth changing. Visualize your ideal life. Go for the whole dream! How would you really like to live? Where? With whom? Doing what?

Don't say it's impossible. Where there's a will, there's a way. Focus on that life; on that person you want to be. Keep the dream in mind and then think about the steps it would take to get you there. Write them down.

Don't be embarrassed to dream big. Things get accomplished step by step, not in one swoop. And dreams are the first step.

Suppose you're a secretary but you really want to be the next Madonna. Can you sing? Dream big, but be realistic about your talents and abilities. If you're a singing secretary, where do you start?

Sing everywhere! Join the church choir; join the community chorus. Volunteer to sing at weddings (and funerals). Join a theater group and audition for all the musicals. Make sure everyone you know is aware of your talent and your wish to perform. If you have money, hire a voice coach. If you don't have money, find a coach and barter. Maybe you could baby-sit or clean the house or teach tennis in exchange for voice lessons. Go to the library and research music agents. Start putting yourself in the spotlight.

What have you got to lose? What if you really don't want to try because you could fail? If everyone knew that you failed, what would they say?

Failure. What does that mean? If you don't accomplish what you set out to do, you fail, right? Christopher Columbus set out to find a new route to India. Instead he discovered America. Did he fail? You bet! The guy did not do what he set out to do. And you may not, either. On your way to one goal, you may discover another. You may pocket the red ball instead of the blue. What you're doing is gaining experience. You're learning and changing and growing. We do not always go straight from A to B. Getting to B is not the problem. Sometimes getting off you're "A" is!

Say you're a computer programmer. You dream about playing major league baseball, but you're forty. You wish you were a teenager again. You wish you'd gone all out back then. What can you do now? I'll tell you—so that when you're sixty, you won't wish you were forty to make a move.

Get off you're A! Assess your talents and make a list of all the ways you could be involved in major league baseball using the computer skills you now have. Research job opportunities connected with major leagues and stadiums. Decide whether you really need to relocate to get yourself involved in the sports world. Call every sports freak and jock friend you know looking for leads and connections.

No one can possibly help you achieve your goal if it's a secret daydream! You have to decide what's really important and what isn't; what's a real goal and what's a fantasy. Then move on it.

A Life Examined—Walt Disney

Walt Disney did not grow up with the vision of creating Disneyland. He was a poor kid who got up at 4:30 in the morning so he could get his newspapers delivered before school started. He lived in a small four-room apartment in Kansas City with his parents and four brothers and sisters.

Times were tough. If there was ever any extra money, Walt would escape to the vaudeville shows or go watch the new "motion" pictures. He used the little free time he had to draw and doodle and perform funny skits to amuse his little sister.

By the time he was in high school, he knew what he was going to do with his life—he was going to be a political cartoonist with one of the city newspapers. So he drew for his high school paper. He did caricatures of the patrons at the neighborhood barbershop. He even managed to study art three nights a week while he was going to high school and working as a handyman in a jelly factory.

But World War I interfered with Disney's dreams of a hotshot newspaper job in Kansas. While he was still seventeen, he found himself in France serving with the American Ambulance Corps. He continued sketching satirical cartoons, and when he returned to the States, he made the rounds of all the local newspaper offices.

No one was impressed. But Disney persisted in trying to find a job where he could draw, and finally he was hired for $50 a month as an apprentice to two commercial artists. His job was to draw rough drafts of ads for farm supplies—a far cry from Mickey Mouse!

But Disney was energetic and eager, and his whimsical flair paid off. He was promoted to doing the artwork for weekly theater programs. The dream to draw and to get paid for it was still alive and well. It just wasn't working out exactly the way he had envisioned it.

A Life Examined—Milton Hershey

Milton Hershey's story is similar. He certainly didn't dream of owning a chocolate empire. In fact, when he was a child during the Civil War, chocolate was not a familiar candy. Ice cream was the big treat of the time, and caramels were the candy in demand.

Hershey's childhood dream was a move back to his original family home in Pennsylvania (now known as Hershey, Pennsylvania. His father was a jack-of-all-trades, master-of-none who had managed to lose the family farm and move his family three times before Hershey started school. Even though he was just a little kid, Hershey knew how to get back to that first house he'd lived in, he'd need money. At the mature age of six, whenever he could sneak away from home, he'd gather the coal that had spilled along the railroad track and sell it to the townspeople for a penny a pail-full.

Eventually his parents discovered his entrepreneurship, and it influenced their decision to return to the community where Milton was born. Obviously his hard work and single-minded focus had paid off. He learned that lesson early and never forgot it.

When he was twelve, he was apprenticed to a printer. Even though Milton was a hard worker and possessed a great curiosity about the world around him, he was adolescently clumsy and not particularly fond of scholarly pursuits. He hated the printing trade. But because his parents had invested good money in this opportunity for him, he used his mother's favorite maximum: "A Hershey never quits."

Unfortunately (or perhaps for candy lovers, fortunately), Hershey didn't have to quit. After knocking over a whole tray of type, then losing his hat in the press (which immediately jammed up), Milton was curtly dismissed.

After this failure, Milton's mother found her son an apprenticeship with Joseph Royner, Lancaster's leading confectioner and ice cream maker. Hershey loved it; this was exactly what he wanted to do! He spent four years learning about mixing and flavoring, cleanliness and honesty. He was such a good worker, doing more than he was ever asked, anticipating needs, experimenting with new ideas, that his boss expressed his admiration for Milton by naming his own first born son Milton, also. Hershey was not only flattered, but determined not to disappoint his teacher and friend. He was going to strike out on his own and become the best caramel maker around.

My Life Examined

When I was in junior high school, I started a lawn mowing business. I didn't want to work for anyone else. I wanted to be in charge. I also had no intention of sharing my profits. By the end of my first summer, I had fifteen regular clients.

Unfortunately, you can't mow grass on Long Island in the winter. I had to think of an indoor moneymaking business I could do after school and on weekends. Somehow it came to me that people who are fussy about their outdoor grounds would be equally fussy in the winter about their indoor grounds—i.e., their floors. I decided to start a floor-waxing business. With the money I'd saved from cutting grass, and a loan from my parents, I bought the equipment I needed. I didn't drive yet, so my parents drove me and my polisher to weekly jobs. I charged a dollar a floor. It only cost me about twenty-five cents in overhead, plus my time, and of course, I had to wax my parents' floors for free. The floor waxing became a year-round business and I made money all through high school.

When I graduated, my uncle got me into the electrical workers' union in New York City. I was going to make $2.15 an hour that summer, and all I had to do was lug steel cable up 50 flights of stairs.

The first exhausting day, I went outside on my lunch break and bought a hot dog from the guy on the corner. As I stood leaning against the building, resting up for the afternoon, I counted how many people bought hot dogs. In one hour, he had over sixty-five customers—more than one a minute! I decided then and there to go into the hot dog business.

The first thing I did was build a hot dog stand. It cost me about eighty dollars in materials and I sold it for three hundred dollars. I built a second one and sold that for four hundred dollars. With my profits, I bought a professional hot dog cart and made money all through college selling hot dogs.

When I was through with the cart, I sold it to a local disco. The kid who ran the concession stand there didn't pay attention to what he was doing, and the cart caught fire. The disco owners called me up to see if I could fix it for them, and while I was working on that, the janitor was having a hard time with the floor polisher. So I fixed that, too, and showed him how to properly polish a floor.

The disco owners were so impressed that they fired the janitor and hired me to clean the place during the day and manage the concessions at night. As a bonus, they gave me back my hot dog stand!

The common thread in these three stories is that neither Disney nor Hershey nor I, set out specifically to become what we became. We focused on the opportunities presented to us. We worked hard with what we had. And we never stopped expanding. There are lots of steps between what you think you want to do, what you are doing, and where you eventually end up. Where you end up could be the beginning of something new.

One of the problems today is that we're all in a rush to complete and do everything as soon as possible. We always have sixteen things that had to be done yesterday. We have to stop and take stock of what is going on. We're so overwhelmed, we're missing the opportunities.

"Everybody gets so much information all day long that they lose their common sense."

Gertrude Stein

Focusing is the ability to zero in on one specific target. For example, imagine you're at the rifle range competing with an expert marksman. There are 10 bull's-eyes to hit, and you have 50 bullets. Your 50 bullets are in a machine gun. When you press the trigger, the bullets whiz out, one after another. Chances are you'll hit two or three or maybe even half the bull's-eyes because of the sheer quantity of bullets. But the expert marksman chooses an appropriate weapon and carefully aims one shot at a time, and he hits them all.

"It seems essential, in relationships and all tasks, that we concentrate only on what is most significant and important"

Soren Kierkegaard

FOCUS ON THE IMPORTANT THINGS

Just what are the important things in your life? After the necessities are taken care of, what is your life about? What is important to you?

Consider the possibilities. Are your children important? Your spouse? Your family? Your pets?

Your job? Your boat? Your house? Are your ideals important? Your morals? Your religion? Your political philosophy? Is making money important to you? What do you do with your time? How do you fill your day? If you had more time, what would you do with it?

Part of the process of focusing is tuning into your own needs and wants. If you can't be honest with yourself here, you don't have a chance of achieving a sense of control or self-confidence. You are in charge of how you use your time. The choices are all yours.

Don't say your marriage is most important if you spend most of your time at work under the guise of supporting your family. You're kidding yourself. You're spending all your time working because that's where you feel good, that's where your ego gets stroked, and maybe that's where you go to escape from family pressures.

Don't say your job is most important if you take off as much time as possible and/or daydream away the hours while at work. Obviously, you don't want to be there. You're unhappy with your work and escaping from it as often as you can. Focus on why. Is it the job itself, the atmosphere, the boss, the boredom? Have you been at the same job for many years and afraid to start something new because it will mean a cut in pay? What kind of job would hold your attention? Do you really want a job at all?

It's hard to be honest with yourself, but you can't begin to know what you want or where you're going if you are saying one thing and doing another. You have to know who you are and what you want. You have to listen to yourself. Isn't it incredible that you can even lie to yourself? You don't like being lied to, but how about when the liar is YOU? Don't put up with that type of thinking from yourself. And don't live a life that someone else wants for you. What does your mother want for you? Your spouse? Your best friend? It doesn't matter. All that matters is what you want.

When you honestly know what is important to you, when you listen to your inner self, when you understand that you are in control of your life, you can begin to make things work for you.

Common sense tells you that you won't ever feel good about yourself if you're living a lie. Productivity is directly proportionate to self-confidence. Achievers keep achieving.

FOCUS ON PROBLEMS

So you've figured out what's important to you. Surrounding what's important to you are quite a few problems; they seem overwhelming. Write them down.

You want to focus on your problems, now write them down.

> *"When you write down your ideas you automatically focus your full attention on them. Few if any of us can write one thought and think another at the same time. Thus a pencil and paper make excellent concentration tools."*
>
> Michael Leboeuf

Now focus on each problem. You can only focus on one at a time. Avoiding any of the problems means they won't get solved. Take the first one and tackle it.

Ask yourself first, "Is this within my power to solve?" Hunger and world peace are probably not under your power to solve, unless you are the President of the United States or you are in charge of the United Nations (and still, they're probably not within your power to solve).

Second, define the problem by writing it down so that you can be sure you can see it correctly.

Third, decide what to do.

Finally, take action!

Let's look a little further into defining and deciding so that we can focus even better on solving our problems.

DEFINE AND DECIDE (And move on!)

On a clear day, you can see forever. On a foggy day, you can't. Consequently, on a foggy day you focus much better. You really have to look to see where you're going. You really have to pay attention. Treat your life like a foggy day. Be aware and concentrate on every step. Don't trip over branches. If you're sure-footed in the fog, just think how quick you'll be when a clear day comes.

Remember that focusing is fine-tuning, whether you are focusing a camera, a television, binoculars, a microscope, a telescope, or your awareness. Focusing is turning your attention to a specific object or situation and seeing it clearly, seeing it as if for the first time.

What we are familiar with, we don't see anymore. We don't notice our children growing unless we haven't seen them for a while. We don't notice all the spring buds until they burst into flowers. And while our lack of attention isn't necessarily detrimental—I mean, just how much can one absorb? — It is important to retain the ability to focus, to scan with an objective eye; not only to see, but to define; and not only to define, but to decide.

To define what you see means to make sense out of what you're seeing. Identify what you're seeing. Name it.

Once you can define what you are seeing, you can make a decision.

Is what I'm seeing important to me? If yes, decide to pursue it further. Decide to take action.

If it's not important, don't waste time on it, drop it immediately, don't look at it any further.

Stop wasting further decision-making on it. And, don't second guess yourself, worrying further about it. That's going to interfere with your being able to focus on the things that are truly important to you.

Focus and live with your decisions, don't waste any more time on decisions already made.

"When I am getting ready to reason with a man, I spend one-third of my time thinking about myself and what I am going to say and two-thirds about him and what he is going to say."

Abraham Lincoln

LISTENING

I want you to pay attention to everyone you talk to today. Listen to them. Focus on them. That's why God gave us two ears and only one mouth! Do not pay half attention. Look at the person. I mean look them in the eye. Focus all your attention on that person and what he or she is saying. You may have to work hard to do it. You may even have to blank out the rest of the world. Do you really understand what the person is saying to you?

Don't start working on your response while they're talking. That means you've stopped listening. Don't assume you know fully what they're talking about. People can tell when they're no longer being listened to. It's insulting. Customers, co-workers, bosses, spouses, children, they know when you're no longer listening—can you really afford to disrespect them?

When people speak, they are trying to relate a central idea. Do you clearly understand what they are saying? If you're not sure, ASK! Ask them to simplify it for you or to give you an example. It takes some confidence to do this. Some people are afraid to ask, "Can you repeat that?" or "I didn't understand what you meant?" People want to be heard. They want to be understood. Be strong and ask questions. Take on the classic rule in most meeting situations: There are no stupid questions. Ask the questions. Get everyone on the same page.

If someone won't repeat what they've said or explain what they meant, they may just be blowing gas in your direction or it's an indication that they don't even know what they're talking about. But 99.99% of the time, you do have to listen carefully when someone speaks to you. Stop what you are doing and focus on what is being said.

> *"The greatest gift you can give another is the purity of your attention"*
>
> Richard Moss

Is unloading the dishwasher really more important

than focusing on your child? What was he or she going to tell you? What did you miss? Will you ever be able to get that moment back? Now, imagine if it was your teenager; what sort of issue could that have involved in this day and age?

Is listening to the news really more important than listening to another person? (It's really the same news every night, just in a different order.)

Is ignoring a new or old employee's thoughts on a matter setting a positive example for the company? (You should cheer that they came to speak to you— imagine if they never spoke to you).

Your biggest and most effective power in communication is listening. When you don't know what to say, listen. Don't just speak for the sake of speaking. If you do, your foot will most likely go straight into your own mouth. Don't speak because there's an awkward pause. Listen. Communication is not a game to find out who can say the smartest things in the shortest amount of time. Listen.

In fact, if a person wants to argue and you don't respond, you get your point across much more effectively than if you fire back a lot of angry words. Have you ever heard someone who has been talked to in anger stop and say, "Wow! You're right! Thank you. What was I thinking?" No, people usually shut down when angry words have been fired directly at them, or they fire back, escalating the conflict. The one thing that doesn't escalate is the quality of communication and understanding. Feelings are hurt. Walls are built up, and deals are lost. Potential sales are lost forever. Customers become negative advertising by turning others away from your company forever.

Simply by just listening, you can sometimes sway the odds in your favor. The speaker can't tell yet if you are bored, interested, angry, persuaded, confused, or if you fully understand. Of course, once you do finally open your mouth, you define your position. If you have fully listened to what they are saying, it will be easier for you to define that position. You understand what they've said (if not, ask questions). You are now able to respond to what they've told you. You didn't start working on your response until they finished, so now you can speak better about what they've said. You can respond to their question and you'll sound smarter too.

Have you ever heard a child respond to the parent's question, "Did you hear what I said?" You know right away if they were listening or not. If they weren't, they try to bluff their way through. It's embarrassing (and slightly humorous) to see how far off they are.

When you aren't listening, you have the potential to come off just like a child. Is that the way a business should be run—operating on half the information or listening to half the customer's comment? No way!

If I were President of the United States, I would introduce a new subject matter into our school systems: LISTENING. I would make it mandatory for all students to take this course. A trained ear can give you a communication edge. Focus. Listen. Succeed.

If you are able to focus on what is being said to you, a number of things will start happening.

First, the person you have focused on will realize they have your full attention. It will make them feel worthwhile and it will make them feel trusting. When someone trusts you, you feel more responsible. Responsible people get more done. They succeed more. (Aside from bad examples of rock and roll divas and the occasional sport star, how many irresponsible successes do you know?)

Second, once you start really listening, you hear more. You become aware of tone, modulation, and emotion. You begin to tune into what is really going on, not just what is being said. You begin to focus on motives and actions. Your awareness expands. Once you start focusing, you are better able to start analyzing people, problems, and situations. You become aware that there is more than one answer out there.

Sometimes there are several options. Focusing helps you think. If you can define a problem, it is easier to find a solution. You have to remember that most problems often have more than one solution. There isn't one right answer. If the front door is locked and you don't have a key, you can go through the back door. And if the back door is locked, you can go through a window. Sometimes that unlocked window is in the basement, and sometimes it's on the second story; then you have to get a ladder or climb a tree to get to it. Sometimes all the doors and windows are locked. What do you do then? Sometimes you break in. Sometimes you call the police. Sometimes you wait for someone else who has a key. Sometimes you get a locksmith. There is always more than one solution to a problem. You must keep that in mind.

"USING" PEOPLE

Focusing on an individual is very important. You'll

learn to analyze that person and understand their strengths and weaknesses. Always focus on their strengths. Appeal to them. Use their strengths. Let people know that you recognize their capabilities and depend on them. Use them.

"Every person I work with knows something better than me. My job is to listen long enough to find it and use it."

Jack Nichols

Am I saying "use" people? Absolutely. Use the best they have to offer and let them know it. Appreciate them! They'll never let you down. How do you feel when someone asks you to do something for them? Appreciated.

And how do you feel once you've done the favor and they barely say thank you? You don't like it! In fact, you probably decide that's the last time you'll ever go out of your way for them.

But think how you feel when you do something for someone and your efforts are positively remarked upon and appreciated. You feel good. You'd be happy to help them again. You know they respect and value your help and you work harder to justify their expectations.

Trust begets trust and doubt begets doubt. That's Common Sense. Sometimes if you are told you might not succeed, you work extra hard to prove that person wrong. But more often, you don't work as hard as you might because an expectation of failure already exists.

FOCUS ON THE POSITIVE

You cannot change yourself or the people around

you overnight, but you can start right now with yourself. When your mother said, "If you can't say anything nice, don't say anything at all," she was right. Learn to bite your tongue! Focus on what you are saying and how you say it.

For example, let's say you took a trip to the Bahamas for a week. You had a beautiful vacation, wonderful weather, excellent hotel accommodations and fantastic food. It was a terrific getaway. But when you flew back, the plane ride was awful. It was the worst flight you've ever been on and, what's more, your luggage was lost.

The next day, a friend inquires about your vacation. Do you say your vacation was fine and then focus on all the miserable details of your horrible airline fiasco, or do you answer the question about your vacation and tell them how absolutely marvelous the Bahamas were. Do you leave your friend with a negative impression of your trip (so he's sorry he even asked) or a positive outlook (so maybe he'll vacation there himself someday)?

But what if your vacation truly was terrible? You can still describe it in a way that you and your friend can laugh about it.

Think of a situation that recently took place in your life that you described negatively. Reevaluate it. Can you get your point across in a positive way? Suppose you went to the beach. It was 85 degrees, sunny and gorgeous. But at four o'clock, a storm blew in and it poured. When your co-worker asks you the next day; "How was the beach?" How do you respond?

You can say, "Well, we were having a great time, but then it poured. I got soaked to the skin. My hat was ruined. What a lousy day." You could just as easily have said, "It was a beautiful day. The weather was great. There were lots of people—and to top it off, there was a downpour about four o'clock. You should have seen everybody scrambling to get out of the rain. It was really comical!" Now you've taken the idea of having a terrible time because it rained and transformed it into a continuation of a good time even though it rained.

Next time you watch a professional comedian, listen closely how he or she will tell a story. It could be the story of the most terrible experience, but you will be in stitches, dying of laughter, and feeling good because of the way the comedian told the story. I'm not saying you need to be as funny as a professional comedian. I'm saying you need to think about how you communicate to people. It's a choice! Think about how you would like them to feel after your story is told.

People want to share good times with you. Common sense tells you nobody wants to share bad times. Try to relate your trying times as amusing adventures. Or don't mention them at all.

We all gravitate toward positive people, to those whose cups are half full, not half empty (if you are not gravitating toward positive people, you have a very long, painful, and ultimately lonely road ahead of you—or a fantastic career in psychology).

The fact that you had a flat tire on your way to the airport and missed your flight to Chicago for an important two o'clock presentation is only a tragedy if you present it as such.

If you constantly complain about your problems,

you will be perceived as a negative, incompetent person. Somehow things always go wrong for you; you lead a life of excuses. You have to put your problems in perspective. Having a flat tire and missing your flight could make a very amusing story. You'd laugh if you saw it on "Friends." It's not the end of the world. You must have looked pretty funny in your good clothes stuck on the parkway without a spare! (Common sense would have put a spare in there). How did you ever get out of that jam? What happened to the people waiting in Chicago?

Having a positive view of things makes adapting to life's unanticipated quirks much easier.

Remember, things can always be worse! By putting your tire problem into perspective, you can focus on the important things in your life.

POSITIVE ATTRACTS POSITIVE

How does a loser become a winner? How do you change the cycle? First, you have to want to change. Start by focusing on yourself and how you're treating others. Change your negative outlook to a positive one. Self-control is important. You can train your mind to think a certain way. You can reprogram yourself! You won't turn into an optimist overnight, but once you try to control your attitude, you will become more and more positive. And positive attracts positive.

"Every year of my life I grow more convinced that it is wisest and best to fix our attention on the beautiful and the good, and dwell as little as possible on the evil and the false."

Richard Cecil

Don't be on the defensive all the time either. You usually don't win a chess game by playing defensively. Be aggressive. Don't get backed into a corner. Know when to quit; when to bite your tongue. There's a lot to be said for persistence, but you have to know when an effort is fruitless. Don't back away from problems, but be sure you've focused on the problem. Sometimes we make assumptions when we should be asking for facts or clarification. Be aware of what's happening around you. Ask questions. Listen. Listen to yourself.

And remember, it's those foggy days—the times when you don't know where you're heading or what the next step will bring—your opportunities to focus most intensely on those problems. If you can focus when times are troubled, think how poised you'll be when things are going well for you! Being well focused and in tune, your common sense will arise, the timing will be right, and success will be just an opportunity away.

SUMMARY

Learning to focus builds your common sense and sense of timing and increases your opportunities for success. To increase your depth of focus, keep in mind the following.

When to Focus

Understand when you're running on autopilot and you've stopped focusing. If you're in a rut or in a negative habit, change something in your routine. Shake yourself up. Focus on what's going on.

Visualizing

What would you like to be doing? Why aren't you

pursuing it? Get off your "A." What have you got to lose? You might fail, but you can chalk it up to a learning experience.

Focus on the Important Things

So what's really important to you? Sit down and really figure it out. Stop wasting time on the things that don't really matter to you.

Focus on Problems

Write down your problems. Tackle one of them at a time. Don't avoid them. Really take a look at a problem and try to see it for what it is.

Define and Decide (And Move On!)

Take that problem you're working on and focusing further on it, define it. Then, make a decision and take action on it, move on and don't second guess yourself.

Listening

When someone is talking to you, stop preparing what you're going to say to them next—you'll miss half their conversation, which is like getting half the information. How can you properly respond having only heard half the information? People can sense when they don't have your full attention—it's very rude. You wouldn't do that to your customers, so don't do it to the members of your family. Learn to discipline yourself to listen.

"Using" People

Yes, use people for their strengths. Don't focus on their weaknesses. If you use them for their strengths, they will feel appreciated and will move mountains for you.

Focus on the Positive

Are you a complainer? Do you focus on the bad things that have happened? No one is going to want to listen to you if you keep it up. Start figuring out how to tell positive stories with more humor. Challenge yourself. Focus on what you say and how you say it. Don't chase people away.

Positive Attracts Positive

Re-program yourself to be a winner and to think like a winner. Discipline yourself and utilize your focus skills.

CHAPTER 4
Self-Confidence

"Those who wish to transform the world must be able to transform themselves."

Konrad Heiden

"One important key to success is self-confidence. An important key to self confidence is preparation."

Arthur Ashe

"No one can make you feel inferior without your consent."

Eleanor Roosevelt

Some people seem to be born with self-confidence. They always know what to say. They always look good. They succeed at what they try to do. How come? What is it about them?

First of all, they work at it. Sometimes what seems effortless has taken years of trial and error.

Secondly, they believe in themselves. They don't expect to do poorly. They persist until they master whatever they're trying to do.

"It takes twenty years to become an overnight success."

Eddie Cantor

Remember, there are no overnight successes. There are no "instant winners."

When you read newspaper articles about people who've won tons of money in a lottery, have any of them been first-time players? No! They've been buying ten tickets a week and playing the same numbers for years. They have been persistent.

Famous film star Harrison Ford was seemingly an "overnight success" with the first and subsequent Star Wars movies. What you may not know is that he had actually been acting since the late '60s, supporting his fledgling career doing carpentry. One of those carpentry jobs for a casting director friend got him an acting gig in George Lucas' American Graffiti. Persistence, patience and timing eventually brought Ford phenomenal success.

Anything you do is like that lottery win, whether we're talking grades, jobs or even looking good. To get the grades, you have to study every night. To get the good jobs, you have to look for a job and go out on many interviews. To look good, you have to take the steps to make yourself look good. You can help weigh the odds in your favor, but you have to try to succeed. You have to buy the tickets! You have to take those initial mandatory steps. If you don't, you won't win.

Successful people usually focus on the positive. When you talk to them, you hear all sorts of good things, but you don't hear the gripes, fears and uncertainties. You don't hear about what they didn't do; you hear about what they did do. These are interesting people. They do things. They make things happen. They are looking for the things they do to click and expect things to click. They don't expect or discuss failing and they don't spend time obsessing over why their last action failed.

What do you say when you come home from work and your spouse says, "Hi honey! How was your day?" Do you launch into an amusing story of the day's events or perfunctorily reply, "The usual"?

Are you guilty of one-word responses? What a boring life you lead!

Didn't anything happen to you at all today? What did you do for those eight hours? You know, if your life isn't interesting to you, it won't be of interest to anyone else either. And if you're not doing anything interesting, that's a clear sign you're not working on anything that will move you forward. You're stuck. You're probably not feeling too good about yourself. Your self-confidence is just barely there.

You must make an effort to move toward a positive self-image, both in how you look and what you say. Don't settle for the same life everyone else has. Don't settle for being stuck. Remember: you are unique! There is no one else exactly like you in the whole world! You are one-of-a-kind!

That doesn't mean you're perfect just the way you are. It doesn't mean you can't be improved. Everyone needs to keep learning, growing, and changing. You can be what you want to be. But it won't happen overnight—and it won't happen without effort. And only you can be you.

How do you get self-confidence? Where do you

begin? Wouldn't it be easy if you could just go buy some?

Self-confidence, like charity, begins at home. Or in this case, it begins with you; your image, your body.

DRESS FOR SUCCESS

The first step to being self-confident (successful) is looking confident.

When you put on your best clothes, don't you just feel better about yourself? All you did was put on nice clothes. That's it. When you like the way you look, you feel good. You feel secure, comfortable, and confident. You feel capable and therefore you are capable. You have the ability to make yourself look good. Once you are able to do that, you are ready to do a lot more.

How do successful people look? Are they sloppy, dirty, droopy, and thrown together? Do they look like they grabbed whatever was lying on the closet floor?

Of course not. They look clean and neat. They look unfrazzled. They look like they're in control, even when they're out of sorts.

You can look that way too. You are what you wear in today's society. It goes a lot further than just not wearing jeans when you go for a job interview. There are books devoted to teaching you how to dress. But before you even consider what to wear, take a look at the body your clothes are going on.

Start each day as a fresh new beginning.

The best place to start fresh is in the shower. As you shampoo your hair, focus on your plans for the day. Think about one specific thing you are going to accomplish—your main goal for the day. It doesn't have to be signing a million-dollar account. It can be as simple as organizing all the papers on your desk or phoning four people you haven't had time for. Don't think about the impossible when planning a daily goal. Think about what you can do today as a positive step toward that "impossible" dream.

Imagine doing whatever your chosen task is. Think about how good you're going to feel to get it taken care of. Use your shower time to mentally groom yourself for success!

Clean hair is good, but when was the last time you had it cut, styled or shaped? Are you wearing your hair the same way you did in your high school yearbook picture? That's okay—if you're still in high school. If you're not, it's time for a change. A haircut is an inexpensive investment in a successful new you.

When you're getting your hair cut, make an appointment for the next time. If you have an appointment scheduled, you'll go. If you don't plan appointments, you'll be looking shaggy before you get around to it again.

It's a fact that most successful businessmen do not have facial hair. Beards and mustaches are found in the more creative or academic professions. Presidents, politicians and power people, in general, are clean-shaven. Think about where you want to be. Take a look at where you are. If you're at an ad agency and most of the men have facial hair, it won't matter if you're bearded or clean-shaven. If you're in a corporate situation and you want to move ahead, being clean-shaven could matter. Take a look around and see what the current trend is like in that business. Sure, it shouldn't matter what you look like, but, in fact, it often does matter.

What about your weight? If your size is a consideration, you have to decide what to do about it. But your weight is not an excuse for poor grooming and sloppy dressing. Indeed, since by your very size you are more noticeable, you should take care to be more presentable. If you're out of shape from lack of exercise, how will others perceive you if after walking a flight of stairs you look like you're going to keel over from lack of oxygen? Sure, your health and your weight shouldn't really be a factor to your bosses, but, in fact, they often do matter. However, there are people who are overweight, but their self-confidence and body confidence far outshine the issue, and people can sense that, thus making it a non-issue for them and for everyone else. If you don't have that confidence, shouldn't you try to improve yourself so it becomes a non-issue for you.

When's the last time you saw your dentist? If you haven't had a checkup in over a year, make an appointment right now. Haven't you noticed that successful people smile a lot? (They have a lot to smile about.) Yellow teeth? Clean 'em up! Now there are so many inexpensive ways to whiten teeth that you have no excuse. Crooked teeth? Get them straightened. Yes, in a hiring situation, whether your teeth are straight or crooked should not matter. But whom do you think a company will hire when it comes to choosing between two perfect candidates with the required experience needed for the job—the one with straight teeth or the one with crooked teeth? Yes, indeed, "little things" like this often do matter. See the dentist. Take care of your teeth problems. You'll feel so much better.

I won't presume to tell you women how to put on makeup. You can take advantage of those free makeovers major department stores are always promoting. You can take books out of the library to learn how to apply makeup the most effective way. Most fashion magazines have articles on various ways of using cosmetics. Ask other women you admire how they do it.

You don't have to spend a lot of money to look successful. A knowledgeable woman will look as good in makeup from Wal-Mart's as she would with France's most expensive export. The key word here is KNOWLEDGE. It's important to talk to the experts. Cosmeticians are trained to match the right colors to your skin tones. They know how to minimize imperfections and maximize your best features.

Call me a male chauvinist, but professional women look better in skirts than in pants. A well-cut, two-piece suit is always acceptable. Dresses in simple classic styles, in solid neutrals, primary colors, or conservative prints are also attractive. Common sense will tell you that hot pink and chartreuse are not colors you wear in a professional situation... if you expect to be taken seriously.

Avoid big dangling earrings and clunky bracelets or rings. Stick with small gold or pearl earrings. Save your diamonds for after hours. The image you want to project is one of self-assurance and competence.

Men must decide whether to wear a three-piece suit, a two-piece suit or a sports jacket and slacks.

Sometimes a two-piece suit breaks up the monotony of a business meeting where everyone looks alike wearing three-piece suits.

On the other hand if you aren't dressed like everyone else, do you have enough self-confidence to handle it?

Suit dressing is a bit like putting on a uniform. Sometimes we have to conform so we can be heard. You don't want your suit to be louder than you. Stick to dark blue or gray, and remember, if you're overdressed, you can always undress. If you arrive at a meeting in your three-piece and it's a two-piece event, get rid of the vest. If it's even more casual, loosen your tie or take off your jacket. Roll up your shirtsleeves.

"Clothes make the man. Naked people have little or
no influence on society."
Mark Twain

The key is adaptability. Never be more dressed or better dressed than your boss — unless you want his job!

Ties are very important and so is the way you tie your knot. Clip-on ties indicate laziness and lack of attention to detail. As for tie color, make sure you have a few red ties or ties with red accents in your collection. Red is a classic power color. Save those pastel and madras ties for summer casual wear. Be conservative in your choice of colors. It's your thoughts and ideas you want noticed, not your ties.

And don't forget to look sharp for the now prevalent Casual Day, or Casual Business Attire dress code found in many companies. Don't let yourself go in the name of Casual Day. You can still look good in khaki slacks and a decent shirt; not a t-shirt! Preferably a shirt with buttons and a collar. Sure, you can dress casual, but make sure your casual look looks good, meaning: clean, unwrinkled, and colors that don't clash.

Men, you no longer have any excuse to proclaim ignorance on how to look presentable. There are now plenty of magazines out there that have new information for men on how to look your best. Skin cleansers, fashion advice, long the domain of fashion-minded women, are now written about extensively in these magazines for men. Spend the five or six bucks and go to your local news- stand and learn a few things.

It takes a lot of time and money to put together a good-looking, conservative and stylish business wardrobe. You have to make the decision that you are going to invest time and money in making yourself look good. Investing in yourself will definitely pay off ten times over. If money is a problem, find a discount clothing warehouse that does their own tailoring. Ask the people who work at the clothing shop for their opinion. They know fashion, and presumably, you don't. Ask the experts, please. When it comes to fashion, don't assume that you know what you're doing.

The motion picture industry spends millions of dollars each year for someone to coordinate clothing for characters, makeup and appearance. The next time you watch television or go to a movie, focus on the clothing the characters are wearing. Look at their hair and makeup. A lot of thought has gone into how the actors look, how they're dressed. Even though you probably can't remember what was worn in the last film you saw (unless it was a western), the appropriateness of the clothing highlighted the story, which you do remember. And just like this example, you want people to remember you and what you had to say rather than remembering what you wore.

PREPARATION

Preparation is essential for looking good and growing self-confidence. Decide what to wear the night before. That gives you time to make sure everything is clean and pressed, and to see that all buttons and hems are intact. Decide what accessories you'll be wearing and what shoes. If you get into the habit of laying out your clothes the night before, you will never be frantically searching the next morning for matching socks or a needle and thread, or standing indecisively before your closet trying to decide what to wear while the panic within you begins to rise. No, the next morning you will start the day in control. The morning will begin calmly and be marked by efficiency. This is the beginning of a positive day. This is a fresh start.

There are many ways you can prepare for things. Preparation will keep you ready. Preparation will give you more time to deal with surprises.

Do you have an appointment on the other side of town? Leave earlier than usual just in case there are traffic snags. Please note, in this day and age, there are always traffic snags. Expect the snags. When you hit one and you gave yourself time for it, you will be able to deal with it more calmly. You will arrive early to your appointment in a calm state. This will give you time to go over your notes once more.

Do you have to give a talk? Even if it's a brief talk, plan ahead for what you intend to say. Write notes. Don't wait for the spirit to move you, or expect that you can adlib it and come off sounding brilliant. Write down notes. Make an outline of the points you want to cover. Memorize what you're going to say.

Do you have an interview for a potential job? Is your interview suit back from the cleaners? Have you ever taken it to the cleaners? Are your shoes polished? If you hate ironing, have your shirt pressed the day before. Do you have your resumè ready? Have you tailored the resumè to fit the job? Or is it a generic one? How about all the information that you will need to fill out the job application: prior employment address and contact info, previous residence addresses, social security number, references, etc.?

Are you interviewing a potential new hire? Even though you are assessing that person, you are also representing your company in this interaction. Are you dressed appropriately? Do you have all the questions you're going to ask prepared in advance? Do you know your company's policy on interviewing? Do you know what questions you may ask and what questions you may not ask? You could be sued for asking the wrong questions: How old are you? Are you married? What nationality are you? Where do you go to church? Also, be sure you know what you are looking for in a new hire. Are you prepared to talk about the benefits and advantages of working for the company? Remember, the new hire is also interviewing you to determine if your company is a good fit.

Giving a proposal to a new client or the boss? Dress right. Plan ahead what you're going to talk about. Play devil's advocate and ask questions that tear holes in your proposal.

The boy scouts had it right — Be Prepared!

"It usually takes more than three weeks to prepare a good impromptu speech."

Mark Twain

Good solid preparation strengthens self-confidence. I think society watches all the pretty people on television, sees them reacting smoothly (confidently), always having the right words to say, asking the right questions, and society wonders how they do it; what's the secret? What people don't realize is that what they're seeing has been planned for that moment. Preparations have been conducted to the nth degree. Many times what you don't see is that the smiling, confident, news anchor is actually being fed all those piercing, intelligent questions. The actor being interviewed has specifically requested to be asked only certain questions. And, more often than not, the host is reading cue cards.

BAD HABITS

Before you put your best foot forward, take a look at the hand you'll be extending to greet the new boss or close the deal.

Are you still a nail-biter? Nail biting as an adult is like thumb sucking as a baby. If you're guilty of this one, you must stop. Most people bite their nails because they are nervous or anxious about something, and they are not at ease in a given situation. If you don't care about the details of how you look, how can the boss or prospective client believe you'll care about the details of handling a project or an account?

Many of us seem to feel a need to keep our mouths busy even when we're not talking. We can't just keep our hands in our laps or on the desk. If our hands are not traveling back and forth to our mouths, they occupy themselves on other parts of our head. We are hair-twirlers, beard-strokers, glasses-pushers, nose-scratchers, hair-patters, eye-rubbers, ear-pullers, head-scratchers, earring-fixers, and neck-massagers.

Most of these are unconscious habits; we're not even aware we're doing them. Try to focus on where you put your hands today. Watch others. There's the tie-straightener, the necklace-twirler, the ring-twirler, the fingernail-inspector, the nail-polish-remover, the knee-stroker, and the pen-tapper. These people are not in control of their bodies. Their bodies are controlling them.

When you're fidgeting, you aren't totally focused on the person you're trying to communicate with. Subliminally they'll recognize your distraction. Try to uncover your own particular quirky habits and consciously work to avoid them. In essence, reprogram yourself. Eliminate the unnecessary. Take control. Keep your hands and body in repose and your eyes and mind alert.

If right now you're saying that you don't have any of these problems, you may be right, but what if you do and you don't know it? That's worse. If you have a video camera and a tripod, set it up at home and train the camera on yourself for an hour or so. Then watch the tape and focus on your actions. Only then can you reassure yourself that you are indeed fidget-free.

PERSONALITY HABITS

Do you know the kind of person who can never accept or take blame for anything? If something doesn't go their way, they try to find an excuse to blame their misfortunes on someone else. Perhaps they're too stubborn to try a new approach. Is that you? How do people view you? How do they react to you? It's difficult to be objective about ourselves, but sometimes we need to take off our rose-colored glasses and find those faults that are holding us back. We can't correct something that we don't recognize.

Some people are too stubborn to say "yes" to a great opportunity. They want to be coaxed. Some people are always trying to impress someone else or make someone else happy. They never realize what would make them happy. These people are actually being stubborn about their own happiness!

And being stubborn is just plain stupid. The one who suffers for it is the person who doesn't recognize the problem because he's afraid he'll fail. He has no self-confidence.

People are stubborn because they are scared. They don't want to try. They don't want to make an effort.

What a lack of common sense! In a survey I conducted, 16% of the people said they were extremely stubborn and the same 16% wished they could control it. Sometimes we are so bogged down in a behavior problem that we need some professional help. But often, if we recognize our problem, we can change our responses. The person who understands that he has a stubborn streak or bad personality trait can often learn to control it on their own.

There are numerous self-help books available for every kind of behavior problem out there. Take the time to read up on the things you need improvement on in your life. Use your common sense. If you haven't addressed the issue by now, you ought to start. It may be the simple thing that's holding you back.

Alcoholism is not a simple thing that may be holding you back. Common sense says eventually you're going to hit rock bottom. Start looking into ways to combat it. The same is true with drug problems. These dependencies eat into your self-confidence and most often will destroy any chance you had for success.

Do you say "yes" to everyone, or you are afraid to say "no" because you'll let them down or you're afraid they'll think less of you? That's a confidence problem. If you say "yes" to every request you get, soon you will be so bogged down that you won't be able to complete any one of your tasks.

Are you afraid to delegate work to others, to share the load? You can't possibly do all the work. You've got to have faith that your subordinates or co-workers can get tasks done too. It's not self-confidence in this situation, but you lack the confidence in your co-workers to get the job done. But if you don't share the load, you will break your back trying to do it all yourself and your work will go down the tubes, followed by your formerly strong self-confidence.

Is your attitude such that you see the glass half

empty or half full? Ask a close friend what he or she thinks of your attitude, your approach to things. Is it positive or negative? Chances are you've probably been told already how people perceive your attitude. Hopefully, you're seeing the glass half full.

When you are presented with an opportunity, think for a minute if you will benefit from it, learn from it, and get something out of it. If you will, say yes. Take the chance. Take the risk. You have to start moving in a positive direction. And it will get easier as you get used to being more agreeable. You'll begin to break that stubborn habit—that glass half empty attitude. You'll make others around you happy. And positive feelings are contagious!

EVALUATE PLANS AND GOALS

Once we become aware of our own shortcomings and are working towards control of our own personal environment, the next step is to evaluate our position in the game plan of life. How do we progress from A to B? Where does the dream stop and the reality begin?

We all give in to fantasy, but all dreams have their roots in reality. There is a germ of possibility in every fantasy we have. Sometimes you have to take pen and paper in hand and seriously list the steps you need to move from one stage to the next.

Even though it may seem silly try this exercise:

Take your fondest, most impossible dream. Write it down. The translation from thought to actual black and white will help define your goals. Be as detailed as possible. List all the obstacles in your way.

Now list as many ways as you can think of to get

around these obstacles. Don't look for practical solutions. The sky is the limit. A crazy idea may springboard you to a practical solution.

Self-confident people make plans for their future. They don't just wait to see what happens.

A Life Examined—Walt Disney

When Walt Disney got his first drawing job with the commercial artist, he met another eighteen-year-old, Ub Iwerks, who did lettering and airbrushing. The two become close friends, and when they were let go from their jobs (due to a lack of work), they decided to open their own business.

They didn't have any money, but they had a lot of ideas and a lot of self-confidence. They made an agreement with a friend for two desks and office space in exchange for doing some design work.

They were in business for about a month (and making more money than they previously had) when the Kansas City Slide Company advertised for a cartoonist. Ub understood this was what Walt really wanted to do and urged him to apply for the job. This slide company hired Disney for forty dollars a week and a few months later, on Disney's recommendation, they hired Iwerks too.

The company soon changed its name to Film Ad because they made one-minute advertising cartoons that were shown in motion picture theaters. Disney was fascinated with the idea of cartoons that moved, and he was certain he could create even better ones. He researched all he could on motion and animation and with Iwerks, began re-drawing the existing cartoons. The team started interjecting their own punch lines, and the company liked them.

But Disney wasn't content limited to one-minute ads. He began experimenting on his own, and, with a borrowed camera, put together three hundred feet of cartoon which he took to a local theater. The manager liked it and asked for one per week!

So Disney worked for Film Ad by day and for himself at night, making the cartoon shorts he called Laugh-O-Grams. He suggested to his bosses at Film Ad that they might consider expanding to short cartoons, but they weren't interested. So Disney decided to make them on his own.

His first idea was to do a series of animated fairy tales. He advertised for apprentice cartoonists and bartered with them, offering instruction instead of wages promising a share in whatever profits would be made.

After six months of evening work, their first production, a seven-minute Little Red Riding Hood, was ready. Disney thought it was so terrific he quit his job at Film Ad and with fifteen thousand dollars from several small investors, he launched his own company, Laugh-O-Gram Films. Iwerks left Film Ad to join him. They found a distributor in New York and made a six-cartoon deal for nine thousand dollars!

But Disney didn't stop there. He tried doing newsreels. He filmed babies and children for parents (with private home showings). He even made the forerunner of a music video for a music company.

Unfortunately, the film distributor in New York went out of business without ever paying Laugh-O-Gram Films. Disney's funds were dwindling. His staff quit and Iwerks returned to his old job. Disney couldn't afford the rent on his apartment so he moved into the office (the rent had been paid there well in advance). He ran a tab at the local café and took baths at the railroad station.

One day, Disney received a call from a prospective client. He couldn't go meet him because his only pair of shoes was being repaired and Disney didn't have the dollar and a half to pay for them. Talk about hard times!

The understanding client, a local dentist, gave Disney the money to retrieve his shoes and hired him to produce a five-hundred-dollar cartoon on dental health.

Working always inspired Disney to new creative efforts, and he came up with the idea of putting a real person into an animated world. He sent several letters to film distributors describing his new concept for Alice in Wonderland. But before he was done with the film, he was broke. He managed to finish the work, but his investors were reluctant to put up any more money.

So, at the age of twenty-two, Disney declared Laugh-O-Gram Films bankrupt, packed his bags—and headed for Hollywood! Talk about self-confidence...

A Life Examined—Milton Hershey

Milton Hershey did much the same thing. After his apprenticeship in the confectioner's shop, it was time to strike out on his own. He had saved fifty dollars and his Aunt Mattie gave him a starter loan of one hundred and fifty dollars. It was 1876, the year of the Great Centennial Exposition in Philadelphia. What better place to open his first candy store?

Milton, not quite twenty, started a little storefront shop specializing in taffy and caramels. Since he couldn't afford space inside the Exposition, he stationed himself outside the main gates every day with his pushcart of fresh candies.

He was a great success: indeed, he had more business than he could handle by himself, so his mother, his nephew and a friend, Lebbie, came to help him. Within a year, they had to move to bigger quarters.

Even though the business was expanding, the penny candies did not bring in enough money to pay the high sugar bills. Milton had to ask his aunt for another loan. This was the beginning of a series of family loans, for as the business grew, the debts grew. Hershey was working eighteen to twenty hours a day to stay ahead of the orders. His aunt came to work with him, and even his father turned up.

It was just too much. By December 1881, Hershey had collapsed from stress and exhaustion. He was laid up for two months. And even though his mother and aunt tried to run the shop, his business failed and he was forced to close his doors. Disappointed, but not discouraged (there is a difference), Hershey decided to head west and try candy making in Denver. He didn't have the money to set up his own business. He was smart enough to realize that no prospective employer would hire him if they knew he was an aspiring competitor. So Hershey hired on as a candy maker as if he were just fresh from his apprenticeship — and he learned a whole new aspect of the business!

In the West, there weren't candy stores or pushcarts that people frequented daily. The candy made in town was usually delivered to outlying mining camps and ranches. Often it had to be transported for several days. Therefore, the candy had to be made so it would taste fresh and not spoil.

The Denver confectioner's secret was milk. And from that time on, it would be one of Hershey's ingredients too. He had learned a basic Life Rule: You can always Learn More.

After he had learned all the Denver job could offer him, Hershey set off for Chicago, where his father was trying to establish a carpentry business, and again attempted to set up in candy making, but within three months they were both broke and headed for New Orleans. They managed to survive in New Orleans for only five months.

Hershey found that his two biggest problems in the candy business were getting credit and obtaining the constant supply of sugar he needed. He had not yet figured out how to run a business. Obviously, hard work alone was not enough.

But despite his string of failures, Milton Hershey maintained his optimism. He knew he was a remarkable confectioner and that he would eventually succeed. So he decided to try his luck in the toughest market in the world — New York City... talk about self-confidence!!!

FOLLOW YOUR HEART

Call it confidence. Call it chutzpah. Call it crazy. Call it whatever you want to name it; it's one of the major ingredients of success. It is that ability to continue, to persevere, and to follow your heart when the odds seem insurmountable.

Both Disney and Hershey experienced failures and setbacks. They lost money. They went deep into debt. They worked till they dropped. And they still kept at it.

They didn't consider chucking it all for a steady paycheck and a safe job. Their minds were too focused and their visions too certain for that. They knew where they wanted to go and what they wanted to do. They tried and they kept on trying. And you can, too.

(Have you ever tried to work on your dream? Have you failed at it yet? Did you give up then?)

When you see clearly the goal you want, you can plan step by step how you're going to get there. Every day you can do something, learn something, and talk to someone, to help move closer to your dream. Once you make a decision, stand by it. Follow through. Don't be afraid to take the ball and run with it. And don't be afraid to fall down. You can always get up and get running again.

DO WHAT YOU LOVE

Do you really like what you're doing? Self-confidence naturally occurs when you are doing something that you love to do. If you don't like what you are doing, why are you still doing it? It's harder to fake self-confidence when you hate your job. Of course, a lot of us take jobs to pay the bills. We don't like or even love the job. Start taking the steps that will take you to a job that you will love.

Sit down and write down the things you like to do. Think of jobs you're interested in and make a list of pros and cons, what interests you and what doesn't. Sure, you may be interested in being a CEO, but you've got to be realistic. Make a substantial list of cons if you are solely interested in the salary of a CEO and not interested in having meetings, growing a company, shrinking a company, dealing with problems, and being responsible for many employees who depend on you for making good decisions that affect their livelihood.

There are many career counselors trained to find you a job that matches your skills and experience (even lack of experience). There are books that also help you find your dream job. Next time you're out with friends, ask them what they like and dislike about their job. It could prove to be very informative for you.

MAKE DECISIONS

Different decisions bring different rewards. Often we dismiss the experience we gain from an unwise choice when in reality we've won a bit of wisdom. Perhaps the choice wasn't bad, but the timing was. We have to constantly reevaluate what's behind us while we decisively move ahead. Reevaluating a position does not mean waffling. It means looking at all the angles. Sometimes it means making new decisions.

For example, you have decided to leave the firm of Peach, Pear & Apple to join Pickle, Pepper, & Plum. As usually happens after we resolve to make a change, something unexpected and unanticipated occurs. Peach, Pear & Apple offer you a comfortable promotion with an opportunity to expand your talents.

Do you immediately rescind your plan to leave? No. You reevaluate the plan. You now have more information to consider. You may decide not to leave after you have reevaluated your position. Or you may conclude that the promotion has come too late and decide to stick to your original decision.

Sometimes we make decisions with no pattern or goal in mind. We say yes to what sounds good at the moment. Often we're just flowing along with the current, doing the next thing that comes along. Successful people think about where they're going. They have a plan. You have to have one. Do you want to be in the same place six months from now? A year? Five years?

If you're screaming "NO" right now, it's time to start making your plan.

Everyone wants to advance in some way. They want more money, more freedom, more status, more power, more time, you name it. No one is content with the status quo. No one is happy just getting by. Do you know anyone who says, "My life is perfect just the way it is. I wouldn't change a thing?" Of course not!

For the one or two people out there who are content with the status quo, seek help immediately. As Mark Twain once said, "Denial ain't just a river in Egypt!"

There isn't a person who has a problem-free life. No one has peace of mind. It is the one standard of success we will never totally grasp. And while we have glimmers of that ideal—all the bills are paid, our partners content, our houses clean, our children provided for, our bodies healthy and fit—we'll never achieve that state, even if we have millions and millions of dollars.

Even Walt and Milton, after their successes, never felt all their problems slide away. If you think it's ever going to be like that, you're looking through rose-colored glasses. Stop that type of thinking immediately. Otherwise, you're going to be very disappointed, even if you have big successes. You're going to fall apart if there are any bumps in your perfect road to success. Put on some shock absorbers (self-confidence) and ride over those bumps! Yes, you still have to deal with them, but they should not make you change course! Keep heading toward your goal with self-confidence.

The fact is anybody can make a lot of money and it can solve a lot of problems, but with money comes new and different problems. For certain, a new problem appears: how are you going to keep it all? And, how do you keep it from slipping away so quickly? You're in a new realm of problems.

When you accept the fact that you will never be problem-free, you can get on with the challenge of handling your life, bumps and all, with a lot more self-confidence.

We often forget that living is survival. We get caught up in the quest for material goodies — "I want a new flat screen TV!" or "I want a fancier car!" — and we lose touch with ourselves. Technologically, we've evolved far from our cave-dwelling ancestors, but physically and emotionally we're still in the cave with them. We need food, shelter, warmth and companionship just as they did. And just like the cave dweller, we need a plan of attack. How are we going to acquire these necessities? In this day and age, we forage and gather and hunt with money. We need money to buy the basics. But how do we get money? Sometimes it is given to us, some people steal it, but most people exchange work for money. That means we have to earn it.

There are all sorts of jobs, all kinds of "help wanted." You've never looked in the classified section of the paper and found it empty — no jobs available. There are hundreds of them, and they fall into two categories — simple and complicated. The simple ones pay little and any high school graduate can perform them. The complicated ones pay a lot more, but require experience and training. The problem is: how do you get in the right position so you can earn money for doing what you want to do?

First, you have to decide what you want. You have nothing to lose by trying. That's where step-by-step planning comes in.

Second, take the courses you need (you may have to take a job during the day, and study at night, or vice versa). Get the training. If you don't start some place, you'll never get anywhere.

Third, put yourself in the right place. Be where the people who are doing the sort of thing you want to do. You'll never be a marine biologist if you don't move near the coast. Meet and talk to other marine biologists. Join related associations.

Four, volunteer or work for peanuts to get the experience you need. Try jobs you're interested in to find out if you truly are interested in them. Being a lawyer looks very cool on television and in the movies, but more often than not, they're either reading a lot of unexciting paperwork or creating it.

Finally, be persistent. Why take "no" for an answer,

especially if it's not the answer you want? Perseverance usually pays off. That old axiom "if at first you don't succeed, try, try again" is one you should make part of your life.

Don't be shy about going after what you want. The worst that could happen is that you won't get it. The best that could happen is impossible to imagine.

With odds like that what are you waiting for?

AVOID THE CONFIDENCE BREAKERS

To keep your confidence going strong, avoid the following pitfalls.

Worry

Worry is special. There are people who actually feel if they don't worry over something that they haven't earned the positive outcome they wish for. The following two quotes put worry in the proper perspective.

> *"Worry a little bit every day and in a lifetime you will lose a couple of years. If something is wrong, fix it if you can. But train yourself not to worry. Worry never fixes anything."*
> Mary Hemingway

> *"If you believe that feeling bad or worrying long enough will change a past or future event, then you are residing on another planet with a different reality system"*
> William James

Don't Let People or Rejection Knock You Down

If Stephen King, Harrison Ford, the Wright Brothers, Lance Armstrong, and many others had listened to people early in their careers, they would never have continued on to their successful careers.

Not Listening to Criticism

Just because someone is criticizing you doesn't mean you should take their words to heart, but it also doesn't mean to ignore them completely. People who sound critical may actually be helping you, but you've got to listen to what they're actually saying. You may not be aware of a problem you have, or you lack experience or learning in a certain job or bit of life. This critical person may be giving you information that will help you to grow.

Don't Expect Perfection

It's okay to aim for perfection: it stretches you and you will experience and learn things and it will help you strive for the near impossible. But don't let disappointment crush you when the image in your head is too idealistic and the actual outcome differs.

Fear of Failure

Don't be afraid of failure, be afraid if you're not doing anything to try to grow and gain new experiences. Look at Disney and Hershey. What if they had stopped at their first failure? It is okay to fail, but it's even better if you jump right back into the game again. Eventually, you won't fail.

SUMMARY

Having self-confidence enhances your ability to deal with the bumps in the road. Often it gets you through the difficult times and increases your opportunities for learning and success. People want to be around people who look like they know what they're doing. To increase your self-confidence, keep in mind the following:

There are no overnight successes.

Dress for Success

If you dress like you're a success, you will find that you will feel like a success. Take care of yourself. Get a new haircut. Dress to fit your workplace. Get your teeth checked. Find out what is fashionable and appropriate. If you do it right, the self-confidence will follow.

Preparation

If you prepare yourself every day, you can tackle anything. You will have the confidence to face anything, from interviews to interviewing, and to public speaking and giving a proposal. Preparation will give you the self-confidence to get the job done. Lack of preparation will only enhance your fears.

Bad Habits

This seems like common sense, but not everyone is aware of their own bad habits. Stop fidgeting. Take control of yourself. It's a clear sign of lack of confidence.

Personality Habits

Don't be stubborn. Are you aware of your problem personality? Get help from professionals or from self-help books or friends. Change your attitude to see that the glass is half full. Be positive.

Do What You Love

Do you actually like what you're doing? If not, figure out what you do love to do. Your self-confidence grows the more you love what you do. Find out what jobs are out there that actually interest you.

Avoid the Confidence Breakers.

ACTION ITEMS

To help you integrate these skills into your day-to-day existence, here are a few action items you can do:

1.   How's your self-confidence?

Are you taking the mandatory initial steps towards the things you want to do? Write down in your journal where you think your self-confidence is. Write down any steps you feel you are taking to lead you to success.

2.   Make a plan to dress for success.

Each day make a list of things you can do to make yourself feel better or look sharper. Make an appointment for a haircut. Get a new suit. Make a dental appointment. Join a gym to work on your weight and your health. Calendar your appointments so you don't forget them.

3.   Preparation.

Lay out the clothes you are going to wear the night before. See if this has an effect on your morning. Think about where you can incorporate more preparation into your day. Make a list and stick to it.

4.   Bad Habits and Personality Habits.

Make a list of your bad habits. If you don't think you have any, ask your spouse or close friend. Focus during the day on how you can get rid of the bad habits. Review your list from time to time and see if you're getting any better at controlling yourself. Concentrate on seeing the glass half full—look for the positives.

5.   Write down the things you like about your work.

Write down the things you don't like. Consider other jobs and make a list of the pros and cons. Compare them to your current job. Talk to a career counselor.

6.   Think about the confidence breakers in your life.

Write them down. Determine ways to avoid them. Review the list from time to time to see if you're getting rid of some of your recurring confidence breakers.

CHAPTER 5

Imagination Plus

"Imagination is the beginning of creation. You imagine what you desire, you will what you imagine and at last you create what you will."

George Bernard Shaw

"Whatever appeals to the imagination, by transcending the ordinary limits of human ability, wonderfully encourages and liberates us."

Ralph Waldo Emerson

"Imagineers" – The job title Walt Disney gave to his park engineers and conceptual designers.

Magic is an illusion, a thing of tricks and sleight of hand. It is making the impossible appear possible. It is perfect timing. We know rationally that those doves did not appear out of thin air, and yet it looks that way. Sometimes a magician is so good, we believe the illusion. We applaud the skill. We can't figure out how he did it and it doesn't matter. Behind every good magician is a lot of practice, a lot of planning and split-second timing. Behind every illusion is a solution, a step-by-step sequence.

Remember the old trick you did as a kid, when you snatched a coin from the palm of a friend's hand before he could close it? To make it work, you strike your friend's palm with your fingertips, which causes the coin to bounce in the air. You catch it as you're pulling your hand away. All precision timing!

Successful people work like magicians. Sometimes we only see the outcome — the illusion, if you will. We don't always see the steps that led to their success. We don't see how problems were worked through and solutions were obtained. But everything takes effort, planning, practice, plenty of imagination, common sense and timing.

In fact, the first step in solving problems starts with your imagination. Like common sense, we all have imagination; we just have to use it. Use your common sense to think of all the practical solutions to a problem. Use your imagination to think of all the improbably, wild-card solutions. Together, they'll provide you with a great variety of possible solutions.

Imagination is the flip side of common sense, and unless the two are working in tandem, you'll never get very far. You can have the most wonderful dreams in the world, but unless you use common sense, you will never implement one of them. You can be the most practical thinker there is, but if you can't dream for the future, you'll stay stuck in the same place, too scared to take a risk. There's an old saying — the bigger the risk, the greater the reward.

"Try not. Do, or do not. There is no try."

                                                        Yoda

I WON'T DO IT!

Here's an exercise for you:

Make a list of all the things that you say you would never do; not unrealistic things like going to the moon for NASA, but things that are possible — things your friends do.

Perhaps you'd never fly on a helicopter, take the subway, eat sushi, go to a football game, go to the ballet, disagree with your boss, go to a movie alone, ride a horse, speak in public, or wear that skimpy bikini.

You name it, there is an activity out there that someone won't do.

Look over the list, and for everything you won't do, think about why you won't do it.

The answer "because I don't like it" does not count unless you recently have tried it.

Ask yourself: Are you not trying these things because...

...You're scared?

...You don't know how?

...You might look foolish?

For example, why would you refuse to ride a horse? Lots of people ride horses, so obviously they are not as dangerous as great white sharks. A horse certainly can't eat you. If you don't know how to ride, that is easily remedied by learning from an experienced rider. After all, there was a time when you didn't know how to drive.

What about the risk of looking foolish? That's all in your head: inexperienced people look inexperienced, they don't look foolish. Everyone has a lot more respect for someone who is willing to try something new than for someone who whines, "I can't" or "I won't do it!"

Open your mind and imagine yourself riding that horse. Face your fears. What's the worst that could happen? You could fall off and be seriously injured, maybe even maimed or killed. Anything can happen to you any time you ride in a car or train or airplane, but that doesn't mean you're going to start walking everywhere you want to go. The point I'm trying to make is that you must take risks.

From the time you get up, your day begins with risks: walking, driving, flying, taking a bus or taxi; life is full of risks and that is how we learn. If you do ten things wrong, but one thing right, then you gain the knowledge of ten things you know not to do the same way again.

You have to put these things in perspective. You're not busting broncos in a Wild West show, right? So stop worrying and ride the horse. Believe me, the horse is trained, even if you're not. So, for your own personal growth, go ride a horse! Sure, you might fall, but how can you get right back up on that horse again, if you've never even been up there in the first place?

People who are willing to expand themselves — their thinking, their abilities, their learning — will go further and be happier than those who never try to extend their reach. After all, none of us are perfect, no matter what Mom says. You've got to stretch your fingers outward to reach for the brass ring — sitting with both hands on the reigns of the carousel pony will never get you the brass ring.

Besides, if you stayed in bed all day, you'd never

know how good it feels to get up and have a good, morning stretch!

Instead of "I won't do it!" learn to ask, "Why not?"

LEARN TO ASK, "WHY NOT!"

Sometimes trying one new thing opens a whole world of new perspectives for you. The world looks different when you're on horseback! You couldn't really imagine it even if you tried. You have to say, "YES!" You have to ask, "Why not?" You not only must learn to take advantage of opportunities, but to create them.

Accept your inexperience in some areas and set out to change yourself. More often than not, you'll enjoy yourself. You'll prove you're capable of doing challenging things. You're not as scared or inadequate as you anticipated and it's always easier the next time.

What you're doing is building self-confidence and stretching your imagination. Everything you attempt adds to your progress in life. You have a fifty-fifty chance in succeeding in whatever you try. And you can easily make those odds more in your favor.

I once interviewed a professional blackjack dealer. He taught me that there are only so many times you can lose. If you play one hundred hands of blackjack, you have a fifty-fifty chance of winning each hand. You could lose the first fifty hands (unlikely), but you will never lose all one hundred hands. Professional players keep betting even when they seem to be on a losing streak, because the odds are that it will change.

Imagine changing your thinking about the odds of your winning or losing something. If every loss you gained meant that a win was just around the corner, how depressed would you feel with every loss now? A loss means you're just about to win!

Professional players also work with statistics. They count cards to change the odds in their favor. If you can increase the chances of winning from fifty-fifty to seventy-thirty by paying attention to what is going on around you, that is using both common sense and timing. You want the odds in your favor no matter what you're doing.

It is said that if those who had lost everything in the infamous Crash of 1929 had held onto their stocks, they would be millionaires several times over today.

Turn those losses into wins! Beat the odds! Don't become a statistic yourself. In a variation of the motto of Survivor, the popular reality television show: "Outwit, Outlast, and Outplay" the statistics!

RE-IMAGINING A NEW LINE OF CREDIT

When I started my magazine, the odds against my succeeding were about 2,000 to 1. That's because there is a very high failure rate for new magazines, and I had very little capital. I had only $4,500, and I needed about $2,500,000 to make the magazine work.

I knew I had a great idea. I knew I could make it work. It was just a matter of using common sense, and a little imagination, to make the $4,500 work as effectively as the $2,500,000.00. I now have a multi-million-dollar publishing empire, all built through common sense and timing — but when I first started, I didn't have enough money to go out and rent an office.

My first office was in the unheated basement of a

funeral home. The rent was $50.00 a month. The man rented me a room because he felt sorry for me. As a matter of fact, he gave me the room where they used to embalm the bodies. I made my office as nice as possible on the limited funds I had—with a little imagination, and a little paint (paint is cheap), even a basement office in a funeral home can look bright and cheerful.

I installed a phone and I was ready for business. But the world wasn't beating a path to my door. I was getting one or two letters a week—addressed to Resident or Occupant. The phone rang twice a day–one wrong number and one call from my wife wondering when I was coming home for dinner!

Meanwhile, I was spending money like crazy putting ads in the newspaper for salespeople. I knew that one of the most important resources of any magazine is the salespeople. They bring in the advertising revenue needed to pay the bills.

Soon I had run up a large advertising bill with the local newspapers, and I found myself unable to get credit for more ads. How was I going to keep paying for advertising? I needed to place at least two thousand dollars worth of advertising within the next two months, so I could assure myself a constant flow of applicants until I found the right people to work for me.

Since the newspapers wouldn't give me any more credit, I had to use my common sense. In thinking about the possibilities available to me (and there were very few), my imagination went into overdrive; I realized that the newspapers were billing me according to my telephone number. My billing account number was the same as my phone number! After I realized that, it made sense to install a new phone line with a new phone number which automatically gave me a new line of credit from which I could keep advertising. I couldn't charge any more advertising on my old phone number since I had an outstanding balance of $3,000.00. It was so easy to pay $30 for a new phone line and start with a new line of credit!

Now, I know some people wouldn't have done this. Some people wouldn't have taken a room at the undertakers either. They would have taken their $4,500.00 and invested it in something safe. It takes imagination and risk!

But if you can't take a risk, how can you gain anything? You've got to believe in your own ability to succeed! Sometimes you take two steps backwards to go four steps forward. Sometimes you have to go into debt.

I've cited Hershey and Disney because they are great examples of American entrepreneurship. They started poor. They worked hard. They made money. They lost money. They struggled. They lost more money. They went into debt, even into bankruptcy. But they kept moving forward. Persevering. Trying. Doing. Imagining. Risking.

A Life Examined—Walt Disney

Disney was amazingly imaginative. He was always perfecting what was already done while working on something entirely new. Even though Mickey Mouse was making him famous, he had other ideas he wanted to try. Since he didn't have the financial independence to do exactly what he wanted (yet), he signed a new contract with Columbia Pictures at $7,000 per cartoon. But Disney kept hiring better artists to do more complicated cartooning. Not unlike Hershey, Disney had an enor-mouse-ly successful product and a precarious financial position. In the early years of the Depression, he often couldn't meet his payroll. He tried to negotiate with Columbia, asking them for fifteen thousand dollars per cartoon, but they thought he was crazy. When the contract expired, Disney went elsewhere.

Charlie Chaplin was a great fan of Disney's work. He thought Disney was a genius, and so he pushed for his studio, United Artists, to sign this master of animation. UA agreed at the price Disney wanted.

It was at this point in time that a company called Technicolor introduced a way to add color to films. This appealed to Disney's imagination. He knew his company had to have it! His brother argued that they couldn't afford color cartoons, but Walt was sure it would pay off in the long run. He made a two-year deal with Technicolor and then personally worked with the lab technicians to perfect the color process for his cartoons.

His instincts were correct. The first color "Silly Symphony" was a resounding success. Disney's studio began attracting top-notch creative artists, and Disney established his own animation school at the studio to train them.

In 1933, Disney made The Three Little Pigs complete with sound, color, and its own theme song, ("Who's Afraid of the Big Bad Wolf?"). It was a phenomenal success. The whole country was singing the song, and Disney's studio began collecting music royalties. A new business of scoring and songwriting became part of the cartoon enterprise (see how one thing often unexpectedly leads to another?).

By this time, Disney employed more than a hundred and eighty people and he wanted to make a feature-length animated film. He decided on Snow White. The proposed $500,000 budget boggled his advisers' minds, but Disney was sure of himself. The idea of an 80-minute cartoon with animated humans thoroughly challenged him. He knew what he wanted to do and how it should look, and he went about inventing ways to achieve that vision. By the time the project was completed, Snow White was triple the projected costs, and rumor had dubbed it "Disney's Folly." It was released for Christmas in 1937. Its overwhelming success is history.

A Life Examined — Milton Hershey

When Hershey began his candy business again in his hometown (remember, this was his fifth venture), he had learned an important lesson — no matter how in demand your product is, you can't make money selling it only in the neighborhood. Using his experience and imagination, Hershey invented a new kind of caramel made with milk, which he named "Crystal A's." Not only did they become popular with the penny-candy crowd, but orders began coming in from wholesalers. As the demand increased, Hershey hired more people to work for him. It was no longer just a family operation. He finally realized he didn't have to do everything himself. If he hired good help, he'd be free to experiment, to create new confections and to socialize with other business and trades people. Nowadays we call it networking.

Through his local banker, Hershey met an English importer who began ordering large quantities of Crystal A's. The familiar cycle of high demand and higher debt began to plague Hershey again. Another infusion of cash came when his aunt volunteered her house as collateral for a bank loan. When the loan came due, Hershey didn't have the capital to pay it. Discouraged, he went to discuss the situation with his banker, and was amazed to find a check for $2,400 from his importer waiting for his endorsement. The exchange rates were working in Hershey's favor!

The next time Hershey needed money for expansion, his banker suggested they to go New York for the necessary funding. This time he had no problem getting credit. His caramels and his purchase orders spoke for themselves.

The bank gave Hershey a $250,000.00 building loan to expand. Business snowballed; Hershey hired more managers and expanded his original factory until it took up almost the whole block, with 450,000 square feet of floor space.

His chief caramel competitor was in Chicago, so he decided to build a new factory there. In a short time, Hershey owned four factories and was making more money than he could count. The demands from his English importer were still increasing. Hershey was intrigued. What were they doing with all that caramel? He decided to take a trip to London. His curiosity changed his life—and America's. The British were dipping the caramel in chocolate before packing it!

Hershey recognized the potential for chocolate-covered candy. He came home, expanded his herd of milk cows, and ordered a German chocolate-rolling machine. The rest is history. He went on to experiment with all sorts of milk and chocolate combinations. He trusted his taste buds and perfected his creations down to the last detail (including putting his name on every single Hershey's Kiss). He hired his help by instinct and eventually built a whole town for his workers centered around his original family homestead. He established a school for orphaned boys, married for love, worked hard, and died with much loyalty, affection, respect, money and success.

Sounds easy, doesn't it? It should only happen to all of us. But have you noticed the common thread through all these success stories? Hard work, yes. Persistence and money, yes. Money, money, money! Because money makes money. Sometimes it takes a while to get into position—look at how many times Hershey tried. You have to be willing to take the risks to play with money. Use your imagination to dream it up, and then take those risks.

THE LAST TABOO—MONEY

Money, and more money; it's important to point out that people have a lot of hang-ups about money. We'll discuss the most intimate details of our sex lives, but money is still taboo. We like having it, we don't like borrowing it, and we can't get enough of it. We don't like owing it and we don't like paying it back.

Get more comfortable with money. It's just a tool. It's a barter system. We don't want to be working for it, we want it working for us.

You might say your goal is to have a lot of money,

but just imagine what that means. Visualize it. I'm sure you don't picture yourself sitting in a room surrounded by millions of actual dollar bills. What you picture are the things that money can be traded for.

Most successful people are not working for the money itself. They're working for the rewards, for the satisfaction. They're working to win! They're working for the challenge of it.

It's like playing cards for toothpicks. If the goal is toothpicks, you see how many toothpicks you can win. The only person who can measure how successful you are is you. If you measure that success in dollars, then by all means try to amass as many as you can.

I think you'll find along the way that your standards of measurement will change. When you were little, you were busy accumulating baseball cards or Barbie doll accessories. You compared how many you had to how many your friends had. As you got a little older, you stopped counting the number and started focusing on the quality. Now it didn't matter if you had fifty baseball cards, or a hundred Barbie outfits, as long as you had the right baseball cards, the right outfits. So it goes. Eventually you will outgrow your focus on quantity and begin thinking about quality. You'll realize it's not how much you have, it's what you have-it's WHO YOU ARE. It's how you think. It's the sense of freedom you can achieve with a little common sense and timing—and you're only limited by your own imagination.

COMMON SENSE—SURVIVAL TEST

There was an interesting survival test that Green Beret candidates had to pass. It was essentially a common sense test to see if the soldiers could analyze problems and handle them wisely.

In the test, you are dropped off on an island. On that island is a jeep and on the seat is a note saying that the Jeep is out of gas. You have to get the Jeep across a bridge. At the other side of the Island is a fifty-gallon gas drum. However, you can only go over the bridge once.

Next to the jeep is an open-top tube eight inches in diameter and four feet high. It is half-filled with gasoline, but cemented into the ground so it can't be removed. One foot from the top of the tube there is a hole with a hose coming out of it. The problem is (seemingly) obvious. How do you get the gasoline out of the tube and into the Jeep so you can go over the bridge? You can do something to cause the gasoline to rise in the tube as high as the hose. You could drop rocks down the tube and cause the gasoline level to rise. Or you could . . .

But wait. Reevaluate the situation. The common sense solution is right in front of you all the time. Hit the starter. The note is a lie. The Jeep had a full tank of gas all the time.

Many soldiers spent a great deal of time problem solving because they assumed that there was no gas. DO NOT ASSUME! Check to make sure a problem really exists before you waste time and energy trying to solve it!

Use your imagination, go wild, but don't overlook the simplest solution, don't write off the small detail, don't forget your real customer and what they really, really want (remember, New Coke—nobody ever asked for a change, did they?).

Use your imagination, go wild with it, but come back to Earth — Don't overlook the obvious!!!

Several years ago, two young men had to deliver a truck of ice cream. It was summer. It was hot. And on the way to their destination, the truck broke down. They knew it was just a matter of time before the 95-degree heat started doing its job. With the image of melting ice cream, they also saw their profit melting away.

As luck would have it, they had broken down on a main road. One of the young men decided they might as well try to sell the ice cream while it was still hard and he fashioned a sign advertising ice cream at five cents a scoop. This was a novel idea and people began to stop and take advantage of the roadside treat.

This young, imaginative entrepreneur was not about to lose money. His name was Tom Carvel. He used his common sense and passed his own survival test.

Remember the old shell game? Someone puts a dried pea under one of three shells and then moves the shells around. You have to guess which one has the pea under it. If you've played it, chances are you've never guessed right. After the shells have been shuffled around you've pointed to the one you're sure has the pea under it. The person doing the trick picks up the shell, and invariably there's nothing under it. Therefore you lose. How could you win? Is the hand really quicker than the eye?

The answer is: yes. There's a trick to the game. The person moving the shell deftly removes the pea when he lifts the shell you've picked. The solution, using your common sense, is to pick up the correct shell yourself. That way he can't make the pea disappear. But what if he removed the pea even before he started moving the shells? There's an answer there, too. Then you have to choose, pick up both of the empty shells at once. That leaves one shell that has to have the pea under it—and if the pea isn't there, that's the trickster's problem.

When you have a problem to solve, remember that there is always more than one solution. Keep this in mind, stack the odds in your favor and use your imagination.

THINKING SMALL AND THINKING BIG

I remember when two of my friends, Bob and Joe, started landscaping companies. Neither of them had much money to get started, but that is where the similarity ended.

Bob went out and bought only the basics he felt were necessary to start. He figured he would add a piece of equipment each month and grow from there. As money started coming in. Bob couldn't take on any big jobs because he didn't have the necessary tools yet. He established a good neighborhood business, but there were no big accounts. Because of his cash-flow problem, he spent a lot of time scouting for bargains. The cheap equipment he bought often broke down, and there were a lot of repair expenses, costly in both time and money (remember, time is money).

Joe, on the other hand, used his common sense. He planned what equipment he would need and drew up a budget of estimated costs. He concluded he needed about forty-three thousand dollars. He borrowed money and bought everything he needed.

Joe spent most of his time making money doing the big jobs that Bob couldn't take on. In four months, Joe made enough money to pay back his loan.

Nine months later, Bob went out of business. Joe took over all his equipment and accounts and hired Bob as one of his supervisors!

Bob thought small and Joe thought big. Big ideas and big dreams helped Joe become successful. He believed in himself and was willing to take a few risks. Common sense told Joe he had to be properly financed to succeed. The main reason most businesses fail is they lack money. You have to have money to make money, and if you don't have any, use your common sense to get some. If you don't have any common sense, you better pray for some imagination!

DON'T BE TOO REALISTIC — DREAM BIG

Even if your present goals are not realistic, someday they might be. This is where dreaming comes in — Letting your imagination loose!

When I say dreaming, I use the word loosely. For example, remember watching "Lifestyles of the Rich and Famous" or nowadays MTV's "Cribs" and you're sitting on your couch, daydreaming about the day when you'll be in their position and they'll be interviewing you about your lifestyle or your fancy digs.

Why not? It's possible. It's important when you set your goals that you do a little dreaming. Plan for the short-term or the long term, but don't stop dreaming about both.

Many people's dreams have become reality.

Remember when lasers were only in science fiction stories? Remember the dream of walking on the moon, or flying through the air?

All these were fantasies once. Thomas Edison had dreams of making talking pictures. He tried and tried until he figured out a way to make the impossible possible. If you can dream it, you can be it eventually. Swindell wrote, "We are all faced with a series of great opportunities brilliantly disguised as impossible situations."

Alexander Graham Bell had a dream that people's voices could be heard at great distances, no matter how far. Now we have cell phones not only in our houses, but also in our cars, boats, and planes. We have astronauts talking to us from outer space! Someone had a dream of flying faster than sound. Now we have the Concorde and can fly to Europe in a matter of hours.

Sometimes the offshoots of dreams are enormous. We used to go to the movies and say, "gee, there's nothing that I want to see, I sure feel like seeing a comedy, a romance, an action flick, or whatever I want to see and whenever I want to see it—like now."

Now we have the VCR, TIVO, Digital Cable, Pay-Per-View, Net Flicks, DVDs, Widescreen TV's, HD TV, Surround Sound, Home Theatre's, etc.

During that critical game in the playoff, didn't you wish you could see that great catch one more time? Now, just hit the rewind on your TIVO and there it is again.

On those long drives during summer vacation, didn't you wish that you could quiet those kids in the back seat? Now, just fire up the latest movie on the built-in or portable DVD player and enjoy the silence as the kids watch the movie each with their own set of headphones.

Anything you can dream of could be next!

Think of it, ten years ago did you ever think you needed, really needed, something like e-mail to stay in touch with your friends and family?

Dream Big.

Now, you may not have any startling inventions for mankind in mind. Maybe you just want to own your own home. Write down your goal and list all the possible ways to achieve it.

For example, the fastest way to get your own house is to buy the one you want. Well, you'll need another list for that one—how to make the money. But there are alternative approaches to owning a house. Start by buying a piece of property that you will eventually build a house on. Another way is to start small and buy a cheap handyman's special. Fix it up and sell it for a profit and invest again, gradually moving up to the home of your dreams. Make an arrangement with a landlord to rent a house with the option of buying it, so that some of your rent money goes towards a down payment.

The odds of achieving your goals are now in your favor because you've considered several approaches. You might come across one of those possibilities when you least expect it, but because you've already considered it, your common sense will recognize the time to go for it!

It's like making a flowchart; have your goal on top and the different ways to achieve it on the bottom.

Any time you come across one of those ways, you have to take the opportunity and jump on it—that's Timing! Nobody else is going to do it for you. You must get going and do it yourself! Be smart by looking for these opportunities and dream big. Maybe you're waiting for the real estate agent to find your dream house. Get off your butt and do some looking too—they can't possibly know your tastes or your dreams that well, can they?

Plan, organize, follow-up, dream big, use your imagination and, don't try—do!—and you will achieve what you want.

CREATIVE SURVIVAL
IN THE REAL WORLD

Let me tell you a little story about common sense. There was a time when I was down and out and everything was going wrong, and I wasn't making any money. I was three months behind in all my bills and over $300,000.00 in debt. My wife, who was working, had just told me the good news—we were expecting our first baby! The very next day the bank handed me a foreclosure notice on my investment house—the only thing making any money for me at the time.

I had bought the house when I was just out of college. I was living at home and my parents were only charging me thirty-five dollars a week for room and board, but I wanted my privacy. I found out I could buy my own house and pay only $150 a month in mortgage payments! (Sounds pretty good now, but back then...). When I got married, I moved into another house and rented out my first one. A good thing, too, because just a few years later I was using all my rental income to finance my business... rather than pay the mortgage and taxes!

I really believed that I was just in the building period and that it was only a matter of time before my business took off. Meanwhile, I was sweating it out. My borrowing power was all used up. I borrowed from my friends, the bank, my credit cards, and my parents. Finally, there was no one left I hadn't borrowed from, and my only source of steady income was about to be foreclosed.

I had to rely on common sense. I had no other choice except to fight the bank in court.

The bank wanted $21,000.00 to pay off the final balance, but they might as well have been asking for a million dollars. I was broke. Since I had the mortgage with the bank, I knew they were responsible for paying the taxes. I hired an attorney for $1,000.00 arranging five payments of $200.00 each. My plan was to tie up the bank as long as possible, so I could get on my feet, and it worked. While the foreclosure was being contested, I was still collecting my rent, and I was not responsible for making any mortgage or tax payments!

After two years, the case came to court. The bank wanted to work out a settlement, but I was just beginning to get my business off the ground and still couldn't afford to pay for the house or the back taxes. I turned down the deal the bank offered me because I still needed more time. When the case came up in court, I lost and was required to pay the bank all the back taxes, plus attorneys' fees, plus the principal and interest.

I had to stall for more time. Using common sense,

I appealed the case because I knew how badly the courts were jammed. That gave me another fourteen months! When the case was about to come up again, I was in a much better position credit-wise than before, although there was still a cash-flow problem. Since the mortgage on the house I was living in was finally up-to-date, I applied for a home equity loan on it.

The loan came through before the case came up. I put the money in the bank so I wouldn't spend it and started collecting interest on $41,000.00. When the case finally was called, I didn't even show up in court because I was prepared to lose, but I had the money to pay. When I lost in court, I had another thirty days to come up with the money before the actual foreclosure would take place.

I owed the bank a total of $41,000.00 including the $21,000.00 mortgage balance, taxes, and attorneys' fees for four years! What a deal! For four years, I had collected rent. I paid the bank the balance with the money I had from my home equity loan; I made a profit of interest from the $41,000.00 in the bank. I took a tax deduction on four years of back taxes and interest payments, although I lost in court, I had really won! I had won by using common sense and timing!

SUMMARY

Imagination Plus

The first step to solving your problems starts with your imagination. Use your common sense to think of all the practical solutions to a problem. Use your imagination to think of all the improbable, wild card solutions. Together, they'll provide you with a great variety of possible solutions.

I Won't Do It!

Think about what's holding you back from the things you do. Why won't you do certain activities? Scared? Don't know how? Afraid to look foolish? Everyone has more respect for the individual who is willing to try something new than for someone who whines, "I can't" or "I won't do it!" And, if you fall, get right back up on that horse. People who are willing to expand themselves — their thinking, their abilities, their learning — will go further and be happier than those who never try to extend their reach.

Learn To Ask, "Why Not?"

Accept your inexperience in some areas and set out to change yourself. More often than not, you'll enjoy yourself. You'll prove you're capable of doing challenging things. You're not as scared or inadequate as you anticipated and it's always easier the next time.

Don't forget that professional players keep betting even when they seem to be on a losing streak because the odds are that it will change. A loss could mean you're just about to win — imagine adopting that attitude while dealing with many of life's obstacles!

Re-Imagining A New Line Of Credit

With a little imagination, even a basement office in a funeral home can look bright and cheerful. Take risks!

The Last Taboo — Money

Get more comfortable with money. It's just a tool. It's a barter system. We don't want to work for it, we want it to work for us. Focus on quality, not quantity. You're only limited by your own imagination.

Common Sense--Survival Test

Don't overlook the obvious—check the tank for gas first. Don't overlook the simple solutions—sell the ice cream before it melts! Don't write off the small details and don't forget what your customer wants (remember New Coke—nobody ever asked for a change, did they?). Remember there is always more than one solution—use your imagination to think of them.

Thinking Small And Thinking Big

Think of the landscapers, Bob and Joe. Bob's now working for Joe because he didn't think big.

Don't Be Too Realistic—Dream Big

Remember, what you dream can come true, so dream big! Someone long ago dreamed of flight, cell phones, and the Internet—what are you dreaming about? A house? A career? Wealth? Dream it, understand it, and look for opportunities to make it happen! Take action!

ACTION ITEMS

To help you integrate some of these concepts from this chapter into your day-to-day existence, here are a few action items you can do:

1. I Won't Do It

Think about the things you don't want to do. Write them down. Ask yourself why you won't do them. Are you scared? Are you worried you don't know how? Are you afraid to look foolish? Now imagine what would happen if you did one of these activities.

What's the worst that could happen? Write it down. But what if you succeed? How would you feel then? Your mission then is to conquer your fear of the unknown, and to do one of these things that you fear. After you succeed or even fail at one of these activities, write about what you have learned about it. Then, do it again.

2.   Learn to Ask, "Why Not?"

The next time you lose at something, adopt the attitude that a win is right around the corner. You might even take a second to jot your "wins" or "losses" in your scheduler and track them for a month or so. Add them up at the end of the month—what's your win/loss ratio? Think about what defines a "win" to you and what defines a "loss". Are all wins and losses weighted the same? Or are there big wins and little losses? Think about how you look at how you define them, and be sure to factor that into your win/loss ratio.

3.   Dream Big

Write down your dreams in a journal. Don't edit yourself. Write the Big Dreams. Write down the little dreams. Review them from time to time. Which ones do you disregard as not doable? Which ones seem easy? Explain why you think some are doable and some aren't. Then, pretend that Walt Disney is reviewing the ones that aren't seemingly doable; imagine how you think he would make them doable. Write it down!

CHAPTER 6

The Stress Mess

"If you had to define stress, it would not be far off
if you said it was the process of living. The process
of living is the process of having stress imposed
on you and reacting to it."

Stanley J. Sarnoff

"Man should not try to avoid stress any more than he
would shun food, love or exercise."

Dr. Hans Selye

"If you're already in a hole, it's no use to
continue digging."

Roy W. Walters

When things go bad, they all seem to go bad at the same time. Bad luck comes in batches—you can count on it! You know the saying "when it rains it pours". You get overloaded at work, your car breaks down, your rent check bounces, there's no time for yourself. Everything that was going along so smoothly is attacked by gremlins and other more visible creatures like bosses, co-workers, friends and even your own family members!

You shake your head and wonder what's going to happen next. You are juggling too many things and there is not enough time. How can you possibly deal with the stress?

When you find yourself in this discouraging situation, you feel deep under pressure to get everything done. Decisions have to be made. There is no time to wait, and this is probably the very worst time to decide anything! You're overloaded.

Your timing is off! Your Common Sense goes out the window!

When you're not in control of things, you'll make hasty or forced decisions that could very well lead to disaster. You are in danger of burnout!

You know when you're not yourself; you're out of sorts. Don't keep going. Put on the brakes! Realize you are not going to accomplish anything major when you're feeling down. Get out of the situation. Don't dig that hole deeper!

Take a break. Take a walk. Have a milkshake and a cheeseburger. Call an old friend. Go to the movies. Slow down, take it easy, rest. Do a few things to pamper yourself.

I know that it won't fix the problems or pay the bills. The point is to give yourself a little TLC (tender loving care), catch your breath, get a second wind, and a fresh perspective.

Stress plays a unique role in everyone's life. You can try and keep away from it, but like a cat stalking a bird, it sometimes creeps up from behind and pounces! It's a fact of life and you cannot hide from it.

You shouldn't hide from it!

People have different limits of tolerance. Some people can handle any mishaps on the home front, but lose control at work. Others let business problems roll off their back, but can't deal with stress at home. We've all seen people who function under the most stressful situations with grace and humor, and we marvel at how they manage it.

Their secret is simple—they know things could be worse! They accept stress as a fact of life. They work with it, learn from it and respond to it.

Some people even use stress to get stuff done—to light a fire under themselves, to get going on that project that's been lingering around forever, to quit procrastinating and start making decisions, instead of waiting for decisions to be made for them.

As you will see in the following pages, people who have successfully handled their stress have learned ways to manage it: They take a break to regroup and get some fresh air. They identify their problems and prioritize them according to a weighted scale. They determine how their lives can be made easier. They figure out how to break out of the unproductive patterns or the rampant complacency in their lives. They keep an eye out for possible solutions and measure their success.

The more times you successfully recover from a stressful situation, the more confidence you will have when facing future stress.

BURNOUT

Stress comes from worrying. Often you're trying to do too many things at once and you don't know how you're going to manage it all. One more unanticipated situation upsets the apple cart. You feel as though you just can't keep going. Everything's wearing you out. Psychologists call it burnout.

Visualize a rocket going up. When all that rocket fuel is consumed, the rocket booster detaches and nosedives into the sea. When you come to the limits of your energy, you go into a nosedive too. Burnout is when your body, your mind, your physical condition and your ambition all give out at once.

You don't have any energy. You know you have to get things done, but you can't get organized. Your decision-making skills are shot. You get lazy. You get bored. You become a couch potato with the television burning endlessly as you channel surf over and over, before settling with endless reruns of TV shows you never liked when they were first aired or worse, watching ridiculous infomercials selling products you will never purchase—500 channels and there's still nothing to watch, yet you sit there... avoiding the "stress."

You become a poor sleeper. Either you sleep for hours escaping the stress, or you sleep fitfully. Either way, you don't feel rested. You lose interest in sex. You become irritable. You get angry faster. You can't control your temper. If you're a smoker, you smoke more. If you're a coffee drinker, you drink more. You become emotionally sensitive and thin-skinned. Innocent remarks seem aimed at you personally. Because you're under growing pressure and strain you have frequent headaches, backaches, stomachaches, skin irritations... your list of ailments grows longer everyday.

Your diet changes. Your body might crave fats, salt or sugar. Your appetite increases dramatically as you seek solace in food. You gain weight and get depressed about looking fat. Or you lose interest in food, lose weight and look like a skeleton. Either way, you don't feel good and you don't like the way you look.

It all adds up; the stress doesn't just go away.

So what do you do?

PUT ON THE BRAKES

When you slip into this kind of slump (and everyone does occasionally), you have to get yourself out. Your timing is off. You have to rely on your common sense (if you still have it). You have to change the odds to work with you instead of against you. Stem the negativity and put yourself into a positive state of mind. How do you do that? Things have deteriorated so much, how can you possibly get back in control?

"Take rest; a field that has rested gives a bountiful crop."
                                                                    Ovid

Stop whatever you're doing... Put the brakes on; regroup and re-evaluate. You have to construct a new game plan and reorganize yourself. The most important advice is to STOP! RELAX! Take a break. Take a short vacation. Call a timeout.

Don't say you can't. Don't rationalize that you have too much to do and that a break will make you fall further behind.

"The time to relax is when you don't have time for it."
                          Attributed to both Jim Goodwin and Sydney J. Harris

You need to remove yourself from all the stress mess. Visualize the entire negative mess you've gotten enmeshed in. See it as a tangible thing you can separate yourself from. You are not the mess. You are just surrounded by it—like Indiana Jones when he fell into the pit of snakes. You have to step out of the situation and try to get some perspective. Leave the bad times (the snakes) where they are and go somewhere else.

Stop thinking about them. They'll stay exactly where they are, waiting for you to come back.

I'm not advocating that you flee to South America and never return. If your work is the source of the problem—don't quit your job. If your family is driving you crazy—don't run off, don't divorce your spouse and leave your family in a lurch. Just take a little R & R.

Take a day off from work.

Spend a day away from your family—they'll probably appreciate you when you come back in a better mood!

Go fishing. Watch a football, baseball, or even a hockey game. Go to a boxing match. Go golfing. Play a sport with your friends. See a comedy. Take a walk on the beach, if you're near one. Go to a museum. Listen to some soft music (or really loud and outrageous music). Go to a concert. Take the family to a park. Alternatively, leave the family at home and take yourself to the park. Take a hot bath.

"There must be quite a few things that a hot bath won't cure, but I don't know many of them."
Sylvia Plath (who should have taken her own advice)

Go visit some friends. Take a drive (but not through lots of traffic). Pet an animal. If you don't have an animal, go visit a pet store.

Do whatever it takes to get you out of thinking about your current situation.

After having taken some time for yourself, now you can face your stress mess head on, refreshed and ready for battle.

IDENTIFYING YOUR TROUBLES IN BLACK AND WHITE

It's important to decide how to tackle your problems, but before you can do that, you have to stop abusing yourself. When you burn out, you start to feel sorry for yourself. You don't take care of yourself. You feel stupid or incompetent. You feel ugly and clumsy. Nothing is important and you don't care anyway. You know deep down that you're just goofing off. Nobody is going to come and rescue you. You have to rescue yourself!

Start moving out of your depression with simple common sense actions and get yourself ready to deal with it. Take a shower. Fix your hair. Put on an outfit you know you look good in (even if you don't think you look good right now). Go out for breakfast. Have the orange juice, the bacon, the works.

Pretend you are a perfectly normal person whose world is not falling apart.

Now make a list of all these awful, stressful things in your life. Identify all your stressors. Put them in writing.

If you can put them in writing, you can limit them. They become defined and they become a bit more tangible. They are in black and white. You can see them on the page rather than just letting multiple vague undefined fears overwhelm and control your mind.

You have now taken the first step for success.

PRIORITIZE

Maybe you are trying to juggle five disasters at once.

You're getting laid off from your job, your landlord's selling your house, the muffler fell off your car, you can't pay your MasterCard, and your best friend is very ill. What can you do? What do you do first? (Besides crawling into your bed and pulling the covers over your head).

All these taken together are overwhelming and fearsome to think of.

First you have to get your priorities straight. Decide which of these calamities you can do something about, and which you can only react to.

You can get the easy ones out of the way first or you can tackle the hardest one.

Of these five, the car problem is the simplest. You need a new muffler. You can't get very far without the car — that's an immediate need. You might even consider working with the mechanic on a payment plan, if you don't have the money.

The MasterCard bill is another easy one. You either pay or you don't. The solution is not an emotional one. It's black and white. For the MasterCard bill and other bills, you can contact the company and work out a payment plan for catching up. Also, many businesses now work with credit consolidation companies that will help you consolidate your bills and work out payment plans for you often reducing or cutting out the accruing interest altogether.

Sometimes, you have to start with what is stressing you emotionally. Is it time to find a new job or a new apartment? Or is it really your friend or family member's illness?

You have to weigh and measure each stress. Look at each one realistically. Dig out your common sense; now's the time to use it!

Some stress you have no control over. You can't do a thing to change your friend or family member's prognosis, but you can change how you're dealing with it. Are you feeling sorry for yourself or for your friend? So go visit him. Go visit your sick family member. If he or she lives in California and you're broke in New York, pick up the phone and call. Why wait to send flowers? Borrow the money for an airline ticket. Stop being inert! Deal with the situation NOW! This is one problem situation you don't have time to mope about. Remember, you may not have another chance.

What about the rest of your hassles? It looks like you need a new job and a new place to live. What's so bad about that? Perhaps you're just afraid to get out of your comfortable rut and make some changes in your life.

Perhaps you feel you have lost control of the decision- making process. But that's not true; you have lots of choices to make. While it was not your decision to leave your job, what comes next is totally up to you. You must make a plan according to the time frame you're left with. When will your current job end? Can you collect unemployment? Will they give you references? Does your boss have any suggestions? Are other people leaving, too? Talk to them. What are their plans? Read the papers. Go to the library and do some research. Go online and do a job search. Start tracking down leads. Do you really want to stay in the same field? Now might be the time to try something new. What have you been dreaming about? Why not go for it? You have nothing to lose and everything to gain!

The same thing is true for your housing situation. When do you have to be out? Did your landlord sell the house yet or is he just considering it? Can you buy it? Ask your friends or family if they know of any apartments or houses for rent. Do you need a roommate? Go online. There are numerous sites that provide help in finding a place to live. Live with a relative. Maybe you have an elderly relative who needs help, or maybe they need a little extra income, and your paying rent might be just the extra income they need.

Don't look at everything as a step backward!

"When you come to a fork in the road, take it!"
Yogi Berra

Stop looking at all these situations as disasters. Try considering them as opportunities. Take the attitude that things happen for the best. A job change could mean more money, more contracts, more satisfaction. Focus on them as beginnings, not endings. You're capable of taking control of your life and making some exciting choices. There are a lot of possibilities!

Of course, if you choose to not make any decisions because they're too difficult to handle, well, that's really making a decision, too—except the decisions will be made for you! Decisions made for you will almost always lead to you being in an even worse situation.

Not making a decision is like being an ostrich. Yikes! Trouble ahead in the form of two hungry lions heading straight for me, it's too much for me! I just can't handle it! Too many decisions to make! I think I'll just put my head in the sand to be safe and avoid having to make a decision. That's about the time when the lions come and make a meal of you, thus making your decision for you.

"In any moment of decision the best thing you can do is the right thing, the next best thing is the wrong thing, and the worst thing you can do is nothing."

Theodore Roosevelt

Don't be an ostrich! Identify your stresses and problems. Write them down. Make them more manageable by seeing them for what they really are (don't let your fear blow them up into bigger, overwhelming creatures). Use your common sense. Start making decisions. Carry a good attitude and it will carry you even further!

KEEP GOING

During these tough times, don't forget to stay in touch with your friends and family. Don't stop going to church, or whatever spiritual endeavor you seek. Don't stop working out at the local gym or whatever it is you love to do. The things that have given you strength in the past will undoubtedly be there for you now.

As hard as it may be to believe, this may even be the time to count your blessings. Amidst identifying your stresses and making decisions to conquer them, take a moment and breathe in some fresh air, smell the roses (you may have to buy some fresh ones), or watch the sun rise. You're alive! There are people out there who care for you and (not to stress you out) depend upon you. Never forget that! Sacrificing everything for your business and eating a daily breakfast of stress is not the sum total of life. It's just not common sense.

"Men for the sake of getting a living forget to live."

Margaret Fuller

MAKE LIFE EASIER

Perhaps you're life is just way too busy. Often our stress is coming from outside us—work pressures, social pressures, too much to do and not enough time. We have to get back to the basic idea of focusing. What can you do to help focus on what really matters to you?

Exactly where is all the stress coming from? Think about what can be eliminated. Sometimes we give everything a ten-star priority when it doesn't deserve so much attention. Don't try to solve more than one problem at a time. Sometimes executives get tied down at work because they are doing ten jobs at once. They start to get confused. Stress sets in and interruption after interruption takes place and nothing gets accomplished.

Finish one job at a time and make sure you delegate some of the work. Share your responsibility. Make the person you assign work to feel important about that assignment. Maybe this is the time to promote someone and give them more responsibility. Perhaps you can outsource some of your tasks to companies that specialize in particular tasks. Can you hire a temporary worker to help out for a short time, or even hire a contractor for a specific, short-term job? Maybe you need to take a strong look at what you are working on and re-evaluate the task.

Overwhelmed moms and dads at home have similar problems, but the same thinking on the job can work at home too. If your children are old enough, give them chores to help around the house—give them more responsibility. If they're young, give them jobs they can handle. Make it a game to see how fast they can move all the dirty clothes from the hamper to the laundry room. Give a reasonable allowance to older children and have them do more difficult chores. If you don't believe in an allowance, reward them with a special activity. Don't be the only one taking care of your house. Don't forget to engage your spouse in the housework, too. This involves a lot of communicating. You've got to do it, don't back down, or else you'll never get any help. It might be difficult at first; the kids may put up a fuss, but now is the time for them to learn.

If you can afford it, hire a cleaning service, so you don't have to spend so much time cleaning your house.

Other things that can make your life easier: Find someone to carpool with to work—avoid that stressful traffic. Find a neighbor or nearby family with kids that need help with driving to the many youth sports activities—alternate carpooling with them every week. Or let them have a night out while you watch their kids and then let them watch your kids for your own night out. Find a babysitter; if you can't find or afford one, enlist your relatives. Get a car that actually functions and doesn't need to be taken to the mechanic every week. Get a dishwasher. Buy one of those new fangled automatic vacuums that randomly cleans your carpet while you're out of the house. Hire someone to take care of your pets during the day.

Eliminate things you don't use anymore that take up too much room in your house; like that 1960's-era exercise rowboat or the twenty years of New Yorker magazines you've been meaning to get to "someday" (donate them to a school or library).

Eliminate things you get billed for. Do you really need all those magazine subscriptions or special monthly shipment of ceramic pigs? Do you really need every premium channel of cable? Do you really need to be a member of every video, DVD, and book of the month club? Many public libraries now offer videos, DVDs, and, of course, the latest books — for free!

Eliminate activities. Maybe your kids are involved in every sport and activity possible. Is this for your benefit or theirs? Maybe you're currently volunteering to do too many things at your church or school. Take a break. What good are you to them if you're worn out? Don't volunteer out of guilt and don't let other volunteers try to make you feel guilty. That's not a healthy environment and it will surely make you feel even more stressed out. Learn to say "NO" (without shouting, of course).

You are responsible for your own success. You are also responsible for making your life more manageable. Don't add to your stress! Get rid of useless stress. There are a million solutions out there. Start looking for the ones that work for you.

BREAKING PATTERNS

If you had only six months to live, what would you be doing? What would matter? Give yourself some time. Schedule what you want to do as well as what you have to do. Rethink what you have to do. What would happen if you didn't do it?

Sometimes we get so busy agreeing to do everything and go everywhere that our lives are not particularly pleasurable, nor are they our own.

People get stuck in the programs of their past. They do things a certain way because that's how their parents did them and that's how they were taught. There's no discernment involved. There's only the sameness, the static marching in place—totally asleep to new solutions, new opportunities and new thinking.

There is always more than one way to do something. You have to incorporate that flexibility in your everyday thinking. You don't necessarily have to change your ways; just be open to the fact that other ways exist and they might even be quicker, better, nicer, or even just different!

It is up to you to change your patterns since you set up the patterns to begin with. You have to learn when to stop and when to start over.

If you're spending time blaming your parents or someone else for your bad patterns, it's time to stop! Take responsibility for your own life.

I once did a study of a hundred successful people. At some time in every one of their lives, they had undergone these feelings of despair and depression. Each and every one of them.

You are not alone.

How did they get out of their ruts? Each person had different methods, but the bottom line was common sense and timing. Each was at a low point in their life, so when an opportunity came up (timing), he had nothing to lose so he went for it (common sense).

So what opportunities are occurring around you right now? When are you going to go for it? Are you getting back in touch with your common sense? Are you going to let your stress block you from seeing these new opportunities? Are you going to break out of your old patterns?

What would you do if you did only have six months to live?

Complacency

Sometimes it's not really stress or any type of recurring pattern, you just feel out of sorts. There's nothing awful in your life. Your job is satisfying, your spouse is sweet, and your bills are paid. Everything is running smoothly. It's just because you are feeling disjointed. Something's missing. But since you seem to have everything, what could be wrong?

Take a look at your goals. Where are you going? What do you want to accomplish? Sometimes we reach a point where we've achieved the goals and have nothing new to look forward to. We seem successful, but we're stagnating. Where did the challenge go? How can we get it back?

You should have both short-range goals and ultimate long-range goals. If you're stuck in a monetarily fruitful but mentally fruitless situation, look for something else to do. It's time for a change.

You do not need your standard vacation to get your dissatisfaction under control; all you need is a totally new perspective.

Volunteer some of your time. Read to the blind. Deliver lunch one day a week for Meals on Wheels. Volunteer at the local church soup kitchen. Answer phones at a hotline crisis center. Call your local Social Services and give something of yourself. You need a jolt of realism in your complacent life, one that will put the gusto back into your work life or give you the kick in the pants you need to change direction.

FINDING SOLUTIONS (WHERE PREVIOUSLY THERE WERE NONE)

Opportunities do come up, but you must look for them. Make the effort and try to find them. Don't wait for something to happen. Don't let someone else make the decisions for you. Don't follow all of the rules just because everyone says that's the only way to do something. Go out there and make it happen! Find the solutions where no solutions existed before!

Let me give you an example of something that happened to me. My job was to sell advertising space. The usual method is to zero in on the prospective client, then find out their advertising agency. From there, you track down the agency's account executive handling that particular client, then the media planner and the media buyer. These people are in charge of millions of advertising dollars. They can make or break you. After you give them a presentation, they have to call a meeting to discuss whether or not your service is good for their client. This sometimes takes up to six months or a year!

This is all wasted time for someone like me trying to sell advertising space. In my opinion, most of these executive decision-makers probably couldn't sell their product to wholesalers or consumers if their lives depended on it! If the tables were turned, they wouldn't survive. It's ironic how people in marketing make decisions on how to sell a product they couldn't sell themselves. Sometimes you reach a person whose only interest is how many people you can reach for every dollar spent (better known as cost per thousands). Take away that person's calculator and they are lost.

All this is very frustrating to a salesperson. Not all advertising agencies are this bad, but they all have a chain of command you must follow to get the advertising or insertion order.

After going two full years without any insertion orders from some of the companies I'd been pursuing, I got smart and used some common sense. I went directly to the client—the person who has the final decision, the person who says yes or no. The client doesn't report to the advertising agency; the advertising agency reports to the client. So I broke the rule; I went around the advertising agency.

Common sense told me I wasn't getting any business from them—a big fat minus so far—so I had nothing to lose by going to the client directly. If the client gave me a zero, it was still a plus... because now I was sure they had been told about the product.

143

Guess what happened? That's right! The first time I made my presentation, I came back with my first national client! The decision was made on the spot. The client was J&B Scotch. For two years, I'd been trying to sell to the agencies, and the answer to my problem was to go around them! I found out that the agency does whatever the client wants. What usually takes six months or a year only took me one hour.

I still had to deal with the agency, but it's a lot different with the insertion order in your hand.

With this example in mind, always remember that there are several ways to solve and handle each problem. The more experience you have recognizing problems, the easier it will be to recognize solutions and techniques to solve them.

The Success Scale

In your life, you will be faced with thousands of decisions that will relate to your success. Before you make any choices, break down the issue into a minus (-), a zero (0), or a plus (+). I call this my Success Scale.

Think of it as a thermometer, except that all you want it to do is go up. If you are working on a task that thus far has been worth a big fat minus, you've got nothing to lose, so take some risks. The worst that will happen is that you will reach a dead end, a zero; meaning no further business. If you're at a zero, use your imagination. There might still be a way (or two or three) around that blockade. If you're already in a plus situation, just keep going!

Everyone has a different platform of success. Ask anyone if they'd like to make a lot of money. Almost everyone will say yes. But they'll mean different things. For some, it will mean $50,000.00 a year; for others, $100,000.00 a year; for others, much more. Your standards of living, financial needs and material values determine your platform of success.

When you're out of sorts and burdened by stress, don't forget to think about how much worse it could be. You could be careless, jobless or useless. None of your catastrophes amount to a hill of beans in the long-range scheme of things. If you want to wallow in a little self-pity for a while, that's your prerogative, but try to keep it short and get on with the things at hand. You can always exercise some sort of control.

If you are feeling sorry for yourself, it's time for you to pick up a biography and read about some people who have had some real stuff to stress about and how they dealt with it on their own heroic terms: Christopher Reeve, Lance Armstrong, Michael J. Fox to name just a few.

You are responsible for your own actions and reactions. You can change you, even if you can't change anything or anyone else. That is the essence of common sense and timing—the evolutionary change of you—your growth, your experience, your control over your life's progress and how you handle the little stressful obstacles you'll encounter along the way. Go for it!

SUMMARY

The Stress Mess

When you're stressed out, your timing and common sense oftentimes go out the window. But stress is an unavoidable fact of life. The trick is to learn how to manage it and how to react to it. The result will be more confidence when you face future stress.

Burn-Out

Burnout occurs when you come to the limits of your energy and you begin to allow your life to feel like it's falling apart. But no matter how many avoidance techniques you can come up with, stress does not just go away.

Put On The Brakes

The first step to take is to stop what you're doing and take a break. Move yourself slowly from a negative frame of mind to a positive frame of mind.

Identifying Your Troubles in Black and White

Next, you need to make a list of all the awful stressful things going on in your life. If you put them in writing you can start to see them for what they really are, this allows you to begin to limit them—thus reducing your vague, undefined fears that are overwhelming and controlling your mind.

Prioritize

Sort out the kinds of stress you can deal with (bills) and the ones you have no control over (sick friend). Weigh and measure each stress and look at each one realistically. Stop looking at them like they're disasters. Consider them as opportunities. Take the attitude that things happen for the best. Make decisions! Don't forget if you don't make decisions, they will be made for you (remember the Ostrich and the Lions).

Keep Going

Stick with the things that have given you strength in the past. This may even be the time to count your blessings.

Make Life Easier

Focus on the things in your life that you can control. Finish one job at a time. Get help. Find things that will make your life easier. Eliminate things you don't need, like junk and extra bills. Eliminate activity overkill. You are responsible for your own success and you are responsible for making your life more manageable.

Breaking Patterns

Rethink what you are doing. There are more ways than one to do anything. Incorporate flexibility in your everyday thinking. It is up to you to change your patterns, since you set up the patterns to begin with. Even successful people face ruts; it's how they got out of them that counts — by using their common sense and their timing and becoming aware of opportunities and solutions.

Complacency

Are you bored with how things are going so far? It's time for a change. Get involved with something new that will let you appreciate what you've got. Volunteer your time. Get that jolt of realism in your complacent life. A jolt that will either put the gusto back in your work life, or give you the kick in the pants you need to change direction. Show yourself how really good life can be.

Finding Solutions (where previously there were none)

Make the opportunities happen. Look for solutions. Break some rules.

The Success Scale

Learn to measure opportunities; which ones are

negative that may not go anywhere, therefore may be worth the risk because you can't lose; focus on zeroes that may have opportunities available, and pluses that offer smooth sailing. Be responsible. You can't change anyone but yourself. Common sense and timing is the evolutionary change of you—your growth, your experience, your control over your life's progress and how you handle the little stressful obstacles that you'll encounter along the way.

CHAPTER 7

Go For It!

"The people who get on in this world are the people who get up and look for the circumstances they want, and, if they can't find them, they make them."

George Bernard Shaw

"You are what you think. You are what you go for. You are what you do!

Bob Richards

"The first million is the hardest."

Milton Hershey

So here we are. We've reached a goal together. We've explored the dynamics and many aspects of common sense and timing.

Hopefully, you've come away with a better understanding of it and a handle on the skills that are part and parcel of common sense and timing.

It didn't require a degree from an Ivy League school. It didn't require an MBA. It didn't require years of experience in a Wall Street office.

All it required was an open mind, a willing heart, the will to improve your circumstances, the attitude that you can indeed break through all the obstacles, the patience and waiting for the timing to be right.

You should now have a better awareness of opportunities, but the facility to make opportunities happen. You can't spend the rest of your life waiting for opportunities to come to you. You have to get out there and make them happen. Pounce on your opportunities and hang on for dear life!

No one's going to do it for you.

EVERY EFFORT POSSIBLE AND EVERY POSSIBLE EFFORT

Everyone has a shot at being successful. If you don't start somewhere, you won't get anywhere!

One of the biggest problems people have today is that they make their problems bigger than they are. The saying about making a mountain out of a molehill applies to all of us. The bigger the problem becomes in your mind, the harder it is to solve! The harder problems seem, the more stress they cause.

But let's face it. No problem is worse than death. So anything else is just what we make of it. We might as well make it work! We might as well go for it!

If you have a goal you really want to reach, you must be determined that no one is going to stop you. (I assume this is a legal goal). Your determination will help you keep the will power to make every effort possible and to make every possible effort.

In my survey of over two thousand people, 83% responded that they do not always make a full effort or apply themselves a hundred percent towards their goals.

150

Why not?

If something is important to you, why don't you put forth your best effort? Why do you let other things interfere? What are you afraid of? You've already learned how to focus your energies and attention and how to solve problems.

Perhaps we should look at the downside of success. What happens if you do succeed? What is the worst thing that would happen if you put forth your best effort and went the whole nine yards? What might happen to you if you started making $500,000.00 a year? Are you afraid you'd spend it all foolishly? Are you worried your pals might hit you up for loans and you wouldn't be able to refuse?

Don't laugh. Many of us harbor a secret fear of success.

Perhaps if you had the money, you'd take action on that divorce. Maybe you'd have time to write that book. Maybe you'd design that beach hideaway or take flying lessons or whatever it is you said you'd do if only you had the opportunity. Sometimes having the opportunity is scary, and the possibility of success brings with it many hidden fears. Do you really want to live out all the daydreams you've ever had? Perhaps you don't put forth your best effort because winning would eliminate your fantasies. What will be left for you if you succeed?

STEPPING-STONES

Don't forget that life is a series of stepping stones. Sometimes we go forward, sometimes back. Sometimes we just sidestep. But we never get blocked in all directions. What if you were blocked in all directions? Here's the best attitude to take:

"All right, they're on our left, they're on our right, they're in front of us, they're behind us…they can't get away this time."

Chesty Puller (when surrounded by 8 enemy divisions during WWII)

The problem is that often we're too comfortable where we are, even if it's not where we really want to be. We're in a nice little niche and change would bring the unknown. If we knew what would happen, we wouldn't hesitate. But we're all a little afraid to find out. We can get psyched up for failure well enough, but we don't get psyched up for success. If we did, we'd be a lot further ahead.

Did any of you men ever want to be a professional football or baseball player? Did any of you women dream about being a model or actress? Did any of you ever try going for it?

Did you know that anyone can get an application to try out for any pro team? Just call the team of your choice and they will tell you when tryouts are. This doesn't mean you are going to make the team, but at least you will have tried! Just because a person is in professional sports doesn't necessarily mean they are the best. It really means that out of all the people who've tried out and made the effort, these players were the best. There are lots of great athletes who never make the effort to turn pro. It's not their priority. There are probably some terrific natural athletes who have no interest in playing a particular sport. It's not important to them.

When the National Football League went on strike, the owners had replacement teams in one day! Six days later, these guys were on the field as professional football players. They were the "pros." One week these men were selling cars, building houses, teaching kids, mowing lawns, bartending, and the next week they were on TV playing professional football with millions of people watching them! The funny thing about it was that some of those guys were better than the "pros." All of this was possible for these guys because they used their common sense and timing and made the effort to get involved in pro football.

Lots of women think they have to be beautiful to become an actress or model. Wrong! Sometimes it helps, but it's not necessary. The movie and television industries use all kinds of people. Pick up a copy of Show Business magazine. Each issue has casting news. There is a demand for all body sizes-small, medium, large, extra large. There is work for the handicapped. There are lots of opportunities available. It's just a matter of going for it! That's all up to you.

In the survey I mentioned before, I asked the question: "Would you like to become a famous movie star?" Ninety-seven percent said "yes." The follow-up question was: "Did you ever apply for a position in the movie or modeling industry?" 95% said "no." Common sense tells you that your chances for getting an action or modeling job are nil if you haven't even applied for one.

NETWORKING

If you are the only person who knows you want a certain kind of job, what good is it doing you? That's why networking has become so important today. Networking is the process of exposing to people you encounter:

Who you are; and what you do.

Talk to everyone you can about who you are, what you do and what you want to do. Pass around your business cards and exchange phone numbers.

If you don't have any business cards, get some made. They're a modern necessity.

Networking is a major part of getting where you want to go. It's one of those stepping stones that could lead in any direction, but most specifically, a stepping stone that will lead you to opportunity.

Don't ever say you can't!

Eliminate the word "can't" from your vocabulary. You can say it might be difficult. You can even admit it will be hard. But don't say you can't unless you have given it more than your best shot and approached it from every angle. Remember — somebody can, and it might as well be you!

Self-motivation and effort will conquer almost anything. Tenacity also helps. Be sure to give yourself a little reward just for trying. Make a deal with yourself — if you try to do X, you will give yourself Z. Everyone likes a pat on the back or a little reward or praise. Sometimes you have to give it to yourself. Sometimes no one else really knows what you're doing or trying to achieve. Eventually your efforts will start being noticed, but in the meantime, be your own cheering section. Don't let setbacks stand in your way. Use them to solidify your determination.

Remember when Disney went out on a limb to make Snow White, and everyone expected it to flop and it didn't? It was a wonderful success. But he didn't go on from there to make hit after hit. No one does.

A Life Examined — Walt Disney

After Snow White, the Disney brothers were a bit dizzy with their achievement, and they expanded again, building a $3 million studio. Disney then made Pinocchio, Fantasia and Bambi. They were all critically acclaimed, but none of them made the kind of money Snow White made. By 1940, Disney was in debt again—this time for $4.5 million! The studio decided to go public and sold stock.

This infusion of cash helped, but then Disney ran into problems with the newly organized unions. Then there were the war years. The army took over a large part of the studio, and Disney was engaged in making training films and a propaganda film called Victory Through Air Power. After World War II, the Disney brothers found themselves still over $4 million in debt and with nothing new on the drawing board.

Disney wanted to do another feature film—he had Peter Pan in mind—but the financial pressure was on to produce shorter, quicker, moneymaking films. The studio put out a number of short cartoons based on popular music, including the classic Peter and the Wolf. Disney also began working on a live action film with cartoon figures, Song of the South. Its release in 1946 was welcomed, but it wasn't a moneymaker.

With Disney Studios deep in debt, the company began taking orders to do educational films and instructional cartoons for big corporations. They were shifting into advertising and Walt wasn't at all satisfied. This wasn't what he wanted to do. This wasn't what he was all about. This wasn't entertainment.

No one works well on scared money. You can't focus on what you're capable of doing when you're looking at the world through dollar signs. So Disney decided to quit selling out to the business world. He gave orders that all the corporation projects be cancelled and the companies be given their money back. He had an idea about Alaska and thought they ought to send a film crew there. Not only that, he thought he'd go along.

Disney was back on the right track. He wasn't sure exactly what he was doing or where it would lead, but it felt right and he trusted his instincts.

The Alaskan adventure produced Seal Island, the first in a series of half hour "True-Life Adventures." Of course, everyone told Disney no one would be interested in a half-hour nature movie. Of course, everyone was wrong, Seal Island went on to win an Oscar for Short Documentary in 1948. However, it didn't do much to ease the studio's financial problems. Nevertheless, Disney was buoyed, and he continued work on three feature-length films: Peter Pan, Cinderella, and Alice in Wonderland. He also started production on a non-animated feature film, Treasure Island, and began outlining his idea for an amusement park that he was thinking of calling Mickey Mouse Park. His brother was dead set against the idea, for obvious financial reasons.

By 1950, the tide had turned. Cinderella was a great success (the first real film for the baby-boom generation) and Treasure Island was also making money. The second "True-Life Adventure," Beaver Valley, was enthusiastically accepted, and Disney's thoughts began turning toward the new medium of television. He agreed to do a Christmas special for NBC that year, and in 1951 he did another. At that time, he became fascinated with miniatures and experimented with making tiny mechanical scenes. But he realized there was no money to be made in his miniature replicas, since there was no way for many people to view them. So he turned his attention back to the concept of an amusement park. (As you've probably already recognized, those miniatures were the root idea for the oversized mechanical replicas— "audio-animatronics"—that are an integral part of Disneyland to this day.)

By now his brother, Roy, had gotten involved, and they made a lucrative deal with ABC. The plans for both the park and the television program were announced in April of 1954. Disney had surveys done to find the ideal location for Disneyland. He knew what he wanted, and just how he wanted it, and despite the cost, he was going to do it right— right down to the last detail, and he did.

The moral of this story is: Believe in yourself, believe in your dreams, and work your butt off to get there. Funding is always going to be a problem when you start out. Often, the more successful you become, the bigger your financial headaches are. But does it matter? You have to do what you want to do. There's no reason to stop. No one can achieve your vision except you. Setbacks are only difficult at the time; you know they can't go on forever. When you look at the story of your life, there will be interesting asides as there are in the Hershey and Disney histories. Get through them, put them behind you, and keep following your instincts.

Perseverance always pays off. But you have to go for it with your heart as well as your head.

When I was trying to launch my magazine, I was busy selling (or at least trying to sell) advertising space to every company connected with the entertainment industry. It was easy enough to pick up little ads from small neighborhood restaurants and discos, but I needed to catch some big fish.

I kept running into the same roadblock. All the big companies wanted to know my demographics. They wanted to know who my readers were and what market Nightlife was aimed at. I told them, but it wasn't enough. Finally, Dean Pearson, the head of R.J. Reynolds, took me aside and told me that no national company was going to make an advertising commitment without first "seeing my Simmons." I knew he wasn't talking about mattresses. What he meant was that I should hire Simmons, the largest independent research auditing agency — and known throughout the industry as the best — to do a demographic survey of my fledgling readership. Otherwise, I'd never get the advertising clients I needed.

What choice did I have? After all, it was only money — money I didn't have, of course. I dug myself deeper into debt. My wife took a second job. I got the Simmons. I sent it to Mr. Pearson and he called to say, "Son, if these figures are correct, and we're going to have them verified, you have a gold mine on your hands."

So I got the advertising support of R.J.Reynolds.

I learned that Experience has to come before

Results. You pick up all sorts of information and useful knowledge every day. I'm sure all of you have read about a great sale at some time in your lives. The ads said the doors open at nine and close at midnight. So you went over in the afternoon thinking there would be several super bargains just waiting for you and of course, they were all out of anything you had an interest in buying.

Now, one could say you failed to achieve your goal because you didn't come home with the bargains you set out for. But you learned something. You learned what it means when someone says, "the early bird catches the worm." You learned that if you want something, you have to get there first, and hopefully you learned not to make the same mistake twice.

This kind of lesson can be applied to anything. You have to decide what you want to do, and then you have to do it! What's so hard about that?

Now it's time to take the initiative. All the self-help books in the world are only telling you what you already know. You can be talented, bright, attractive, self-confident, creative, and imaginative, and still be sitting on your duff.

Motivation doesn't come from the outside; no matter how many articles you read or how many motivational seminars you take. It all comes from inside. Your common sense takes over and says, "What are you waiting for?" Only you can answer that question.

OUT OF THE MOUTHS OF BABES

Wisdom and common sense sometimes come out of the mouths of babes.

One day I was sitting on the couch watching TV while my wife was trying to teach our son Mikey how to write. After an hour of frustration, my wife gently suggested they give it a rest, since Mikey's penmanship was terrible. Mikey, who was in the first grade at the time, shrugged and said, "Who cares? When I grow up, I'll hire a secretary just like my Daddy, and she can write for me with a typewriter!"

My wife and I looked at each other and burst out laughing. I was proud of Mikey—not because of the remark he made, but because he already had the ability and know-how to get the job done. He used common sense. Just because you can't do that special job or duty personally, doesn't mean you can't see to it that the job gets done. You just have to find someone who can do it. The results are the same!

The problem with today's society is that too many people are trying to figure out what's wrong—when they should be spending more time trying to figure out what works!

If Mikey can use common sense to get to the heart of a problem at age six, you certainly can use the ideas I've shared with you to help you positively and effectively communicate and make good decisions for a continually successful (success-filled) life!

Just remember these three simple thoughts:
YOU MUST MAKE THE EFFORT.
YOU MUST THINK POSITIVE.
WHY NOT YOU?

You don't want to say when you're seventy years old:
I SHOULD HAVE...

I COULD HAVE...
I WOULD HAVE...
BUT I DIDN'T...
AND NOW I CAN'T...
AND PROBABLY WON'T

Remember, God gave us common sense and timing. It's up to us to know how to use them.
Go for it!!!

"Only God knows the future, for you to know the future or guess what is in store for you will do no good. Because knowing the future is not having one."

Michael J. Cutino

CHAPTER 8

Common Sense & Timing in the Workplace

"Opportunities are everywhere. The recession might be drawing to a close, but its continuing legacy is employers' reliance on short-term staff. There may be fewer jobs for life, but there are more jobs in a lifetime."
Lucy Benington

"The best career advice given to the young is, 'Find out what you like doing best and get someone to pay you for doing it."
Katharine Whitehorn

"I get satisfaction of three kinds. One is creating something, one is being paid for it, and one is the feeling that I haven't just been sitting on my ass all afternoon."
William F. Buckley, Jr.

"Work is the price you pay for money."
Anonymous

In this book, we've discussed Common Sense and Timing in relation to business and social success. We've discussed the various ways to find success, to open ourselves up to opportunities and pounce on them when the timing is right. We're focusing, we are self-confident, and using our imagination to dream big, we're dealing squarely with the stress mess and we're going for it. We're putting together all the skills we've learned.

In this chapter, we're going to focus specifically on using these skills to get in and stay in the workplace of our choice (or the beginning step on our journey to business success). Maybe it's not the dream job you wanted, but it's a place full of opportunities to further yourself, to gain experience, to learn how to work with all kinds of people. It may be the beginning of your journey or it may be the career change in the middle of your journey. Common Sense and Timing can take you further than you dreamed. So, we're going to look at the many aspects of the workplace and see how we can get what we want out of it, improve our situation, and move up or move on.

FINDING THE JOB

What do you want to do? Is there a particular industry in which you're interested? Is there anything you're particularly good at? Don't worry if you don't think you're good at anything (although you could think more positively than that). Professional career counseling is the most important step to take. Perhaps this isn't the first job you're looking for— you've been good in a particular industry for a long time and you're ready for a change. Again, career counseling is the place to start.

"The best career advice given to the young is, 'Find out what you like doing best and get someone to pay you for doing it."

Katharine Whitehorn

Career counselors are trained to help you figure out what you want to do with your life. They'll interview you and give you tests designed to figure out what you may or may not be inclined to do. Of course, you must have an open mind and consider jobs you've never heard of before or jobs that you thought you knew, but never saw yourself a part of.

The government has employment development centers with career counselors, job postings, and they have listings for possible training opportunities.

If you're in college, there is career counseling as well as job opportunity listings, such as possible internships which allow you to get into a company and experience different jobs that interest you. They just don't pay much, if anything at all, but the experience you gain will prove to be invaluable. Also, don't ignore the local junior or city colleges, which have plenty of opportunities. They even have low-priced classes you could take in the evening to learn about subjects you're interested in.

If you head to your local public library, the librarian would be more than happy to point out the job resource section. They have newspaper resources for your local and metropolitan areas. They have books on finding the right job for you. More often than not, they have access to the Internet, where you can look for the same resources: jobs available, how to find the right job for you, government websites, etc.

If you don't check out these opportunities, how are you going to know what's out there? It seems like it would be common sense to do so, but don't you know a few people out there who have been unemployed for months, what's their story? Are they really leaving themselves open to opportunities out

164

there? Or are they just wallowing in worry, paralyzed with the changes they're facing? Don't be a wallower!

Get out there and ask people what they do. Ask your relatives. Ask your friends. Don't forget to be positive and listen. You never know when you talk to people if an opportunity will open up. Many people get their next job simply because they talked to someone who knew of an available opportunity. Yes, many times it is who you know. Of course, if you take the job, act appropriately so as not to affect the reputation of your friend or relative who may have gone out on a limb for you.

When considering the jobs out there, take a look at what's going on in the world. If you're thinking of starting a new career in computer programming or you're going to start working on a computer major in college, you might want to think twice when you understand that a lot of American companies are starting to use a less expensive international work base. There's still opportunity, but it may be more limited than you think. You need to do the research and decide for yourself. Don't let one or two newspaper or magazine articles make the decision for you. Perhaps there's a niche you will be able to fill. But at least know what you're getting yourself into.

Eventually you will start interviewing for jobs. Interviewing is not just about the company finding out about you. It's also the chance for you to interview the company to find out about them. Are you sure it's the company you want to work for? Take a look at how the workers are dressed. Is it a professional place or does it look like it was just thrown together, with shabby cubicles, and worn out looking people? Though they may offer you the salary you're looking for, is it really the place with a future for you? You have to decide that for yourself. Perhaps it does look shabby and thrown together, but it may be a startup company and you're getting in at the ground floor. The opportunities for growth, experience, and learning could be immense. Can you seriously pass that place up, even with a salary less than you were looking for? You're going to have to research the place, preferably before you get to the interview.

How do you research a company? Go back to the library and ask the librarian to show you how. Are they a public company or a private one? Are they focused on pleasing stockholders or customers? Check the Better Business Bureau for information about the company. Look up the company's name on the Internet. Did it show up? Were the hits positive or negative? Are the company's leaders going through any indictments or scandals? Companies and leaders like Enron, Martha Stewart, and Arthur Andersen can send shivers through the collective spine. You can't guess with any accuracy whether the company you join will have similar problems, but at least do some research just to make sure there's nothing currently going on.

No matter what the company looks like, you'll need to dress up for the interview. Go back to the chapter on self-confidence for ideas on looking sharp. Plus, use your common sense; get a good night's sleep the night before and show up on time for the interview. Twenty minutes prior will allow you time to fill out any paperwork or applications. If you're driving across opposite ends of the city to get to the interview, leave earlier than you normally would. You can never predict the surprises that traffic can hold for you.

Be prepared. Bring your resumè, even if you've sent one already. Have names and addresses for business and non-business references handy. Make sure all your information is up to date. Bring a pen. Visit the restroom before the interview. Check your teeth for food particles. Bring back-up glasses in case you lose a contact lense. Turn off your cell phone before the interview. If you are expecting an important call or an emergency call, you can mention that to the interviewer before your interview takes place.

Be polite and respectful during the interview. Answer their questions as completely as possible. Don't make up anything. These people often know their stuff and if they get a whiff of you not being genuine, you will not get that job. If you do bluff, just be prepared if they call you on your bluff. Wait until the appropriate time to ask questions about the job. Take the lead from the interviewer. Sometimes, they'll welcome your comments during the course of the interview or they may leave it to the end. If they don't leave you time to answer your questions, this may be a reflection of the culture there—not a good sign of a good place to work. Above all, answer the questions they ask you. Don't go off on a tangent and tell them everything else but the answer they were looking for:

"Have common sense and...stick to the point."

Somerset Maugham

If you feel the interview is not going well, don't give up; don't let them see you sweat. Keep it all on a positive note. They may not see you fitting the position you're interviewing for, but if they see how positive and upbeat you are, they may see you in another position now or even down the road. That's right, a great opportunity may come out of an opportunity that didn't go your way. Don't burn your bridges!!!

A word about your resumè. Write it. Or have someone else write it. But either way, give it to someone else you trust to read it for mistakes. By the way, please use spell check. Don't have any typos on that resumè. It's like going to an interview with coffee stains (or worse) all over your nice suit. Many times the first person you're going to interview with is someone from the Human Resources department (if it's a big company). They may not fully understand your fantastic expertise in the position that you're applying for, but if they see typos, they won't like it. You won't get that second interview with the boss who would hire you, typos be-darned, because of your fantastic expertise. You've got to do everything expected to get by that first gatekeeper.

If you don't know what's expected in an interview, read up on it. There are a lot of questions they'll ask, and if you're not prepared for them, you're going to come off looking bad. There are books out there that detail the questions most interviewers will ask. Practice answering them. Get a friend to ask you those questions. Answer them. Practice them again and again. Be prepared.

If your interview goes south, just chalk it up to a

learning experience, especially those of you looking for a new career midway into your life or you've been recently laid-off. If you haven't had to interview in years, you're probably rusty. Practice it. Don't expect to just go to one interview and get the job. Try to go to as many interviews as possible so you can break through the rust that's built up over the years.

BEGINNING THE NEW JOB/CAREER

So you got the job. Guess what? It's a new company. It's a different company. Nobody there has worked with you. So you can't get by on the charm or the sense of family you've been using to get by at your old company. You're starting fresh. It's a great new opportunity. Take a fresh new approach. Don't assume the new company works like your old company. You have a new reputation to build with new people. You have to give it time and patience.

If it's your first job, be patient. You have a reputation to build before your new co-workers trust you. You need to get familiar with how things run in the company. You've got to start learning to read people. If it's your first job out of college or high school, consider your bosses and co-workers as if they're your new teacher, professor or they are your new fellow students. It takes awhile to figure them out. Just be patient. Just like school, these things take a while.

If it's your new career or your first job, you have to learn about the realistic way in which the work gets done. It's no longer theory as explored in college or in a book. It is the way it is, as defined by the founders of the company, the leaders, the middle managers, the direct supervisors, and your co-workers. It may not be right, but it is the way it is. You have to learn it first, before you start making suggestions. There is almost always a reason things are done a certain way. Figure that out first. I'm not saying that the way things are done is right, but there may be some logic behind it and then again there may not be. But before you go off and say something insulting to the people who have been doing it a certain way for many years, work with it. Learn about it. If your idea still holds true, try to discuss it with your new co-workers. Get a feel for what the response may be.

As you are learning how things are done at the company, you must ask questions. If you don't ask questions, you aren't going to learn anything, and there will be a reasonable expectation that you are learning things. Now is the time to ask questions and make your mistakes. Usually in the first three to six months, depending upon the complexity of the job and if you were given training or not, there is a bit of an allowance for questions and mistakes. However, if you find yourself asking the same questions over and over, your co-workers and boss may grow tired of wasting their time on you. When you ask a question, take notes. Review your notes. I've known people who take the most detailed notes when learning a new subject or task, but then they don't review their notes and end up asking the same questions and taking more notes. It's very frustrating because many times in the corporate world, there isn't time for training and the person stuck with training you may also have a large workload to balance. Don't waste their time. Review your notes before you go asking a question. Sure it may seem simpler and

170

quicker to ask someone instead of going through your notes, but every time you ask a question you are cutting into that person's time. So just be careful and balance it out. Try to figure things out for yourself. A good rule of thumb depending upon the complexity of your tasks is to spend ten to twenty minutes attempting to figure things out for yourself. If after that time you are still stuck, don't waste any time trying to find the answer yourself. Go ask someone for help. It's a balance.

Try to develop a mentor. Find someone who's been in the company for a while and ask them questions. Ask them for their take on how and why things are done at the company. If they're particularly helpful, take them out for lunch. Be thankful for the time they've spent with you.

Start developing your reputation. Once you've mastered your work expectations, it's time to get known in the company. Volunteer for additional work. Get involved in meetings to meet other people in the company. If your boss is going to have to miss a meeting, volunteer to take notes for him or her. It's not that you want their job; it's just an educational opportunity for you to get to know other people within the company and find out how they interact with your department. Meetings will also give you a chance to see the politics within the company: what departments wield more or less power; what managers or vice-presidents have the final say on projects; what direction the company is going in. Get involved. Volunteer to work on side projects from meetings as long as they don't interfere with your regular duties. Don't be negative or complain about how you think things should be. Always be positive.

171

Be game for anything. If you are assigned tasks, get them done. You are developing your reputation. If you say you are going to do something, do it. Keep your word. Don't give excuses if the job doesn't get done. If for some reason you are unable to get the job done, let them know as soon as possible what you're going to do to set things right.

As stated previously, volunteer for all sorts of things that allow you to experience more of the workings of the company, even if it's just to help out in the company's favorite charity. Get involved in the company. Eventually the right people will notice you and the opportunities will open up for you. Even if you're the lowest person on the totem pole, be the best, most positive, open to anything, type of worker. Believe me, it gets noticed! You'll find that so many people settle for what they're doing and they don't want to move on. They get into that comfortable rut. If you show any positive signs of wanting to do more, you will get noticed!

ETHICS AND ATTITUDE

Take care of yourself. Don't say "yes" to everything. Be sure to fight for what you believe in. Set your boundaries. If you say "yes" to everything, you may end up doing everything. You may end up too overwhelmed and come off looking worse. They may also end up relying on you to get a certain thing done and before long, no one will ever let you do anything else, because they won't be able to imagine anyone doing what you do, but you. Then, you're stuck with no chance of growth.

Treat everyone the way you wish to be treated. Get along with all levels of employees. Treat the mailroom guys right (that way you'll be sure to get your mail). Treat the cleaning people right. Don't talk down to the secretaries or executive assistants (you don't want them to prevent you from getting access to their bosses). Treat everyone right. You never know when someone could be promoted to be your boss. Or, conversely, you never know when you might end up being someone's boss and if you haven't treated them right, you may have more work ahead of you than anticipated.

Be patient. Be very patient. If you're really frustrated or angry, take a break before you really put your foot in your mouth. This goes equally for bosses and employees.

If you do make a mistake and hurt someone's feelings, you will do so much if you just own up to it and apologize. You're not in elementary school anymore. Act like an adult and apologize to whomever you've offended. Sometimes an apology will earn you even more goodwill than you even had before. It's worth it and it's the right thing to do. If you've made someone miserable, apologize before things get worse and it starts affecting your job or their job.

In the same vein, if you make a mistake on a project and it fails, take responsibility for it. Just do it. Aren't you tired of seeing people in the news who have made mistakes trying to dodge accountability for what they've done? Wouldn't you like them to just say, "Okay, I did it. I made a mistake." America should be tired of these types of people by now. Denials, beating around the bush, and the years drag on. Pick a politician. Pick a scandal. But in the workplace, if a task you're in charge of crashes and burns, take the heat and move on. Chalk it up to a learning experience.

COMMUNICATION

Communication at a new company is so important. Communication is key for people to understand one another. Good communication can put everyone in a department or company on the same page. Everyone knows what is expected of them. It can be communicating with your staff in a meeting. It can be communicating with your boss about a problem you see. It can be communicating with an unhappy customer. It can be a well-written PowerPoint presentation explaining a new product or workflow. It can be a memo explaining a new policy. It can be an e-mail to one person encouraging them to make a certain goal. It can be a phone call. There are so many ways to communicate at work. Sometimes people are too lazy to communicate effectively. Sometimes people haven't been taught how to communicate effectively.

Here are some good things to keep in mind when communicating at work:

Don't interrupt people when they're talking. You don't like it when people interrupt you, so why do it to others? Plus, if you're interrupting, it means you're not listening—that's not good communication.

Be a good listener (see the chapter on How to Focus to learn more about being a better listener). If you're the boss, be an especially good listener to your subordinates. If you don't listen, they'll stop telling you things—things that you might want to know. In staff meetings, schedule a time at the end for questions and issues, so that your staff can bring up things that they faced during the week. This will clue you in to things that are going on. If your staff asks you to look into something, make time for it. It shows you care about the things that matter to them. As a result, they'll work even harder for you. If someone dominates the conversation with an issue that may not apply to the whole team, take it offline and handle it with that person in your office. Also, keep an open door policy, so that your staff has access to you during the day. If that isn't possible, schedule some access time during the day, or if you're really over-booked, schedule a specific time once a week. The benefits will always outweigh the costs.

Be polite in your e-mails, memos, phone conversations, in meetings, and face-to-face. If you are angry about something, write it down in an e-mail, but don't send it! Wait an hour or so, or even until the next day, and then re-read the e-mail. You might even delete it and start over. If re-written, it will be less a reaction of your anger and more an intelligent response. An angry e-mail will typically produce more problems and get more people (bosses!) involved. You don't want that. Handle the problem yourself after you've had time to think it out and also to let some of that anger dissipate. You might even want someone to read the e-mail before you send it. Listen to their suggestions how it might be worded better.

If it's a bigger problem, bring up the issue with your boss. Ask how it should be best handled.

STRESS

As discussed earlier, there are many ways to handle stress. In the workplace, there are many degrees of stress, and the causes of stress are multiple.

Your co-workers can stress you out. Your boss can stress you out. The difficulty of the work can stress you out. Think of Lucy in the I Love Lucy episode with the quickening pace of the conveyor belt of chocolates—talk about stress! Deadlines and quotas can stress you out.

But what can you do about it? If it's getting the better of you, you better do something about it fast.

Is it time to talk to the boss about it? Are you sick of the work? Perhaps it's time to think about moving on. Or maybe the solution is simple: It's time to take a day off.

What's wrong with taking a day off here and there? Can't catch up with the work? The work will always be there, and there is never an ideal time to take a day off.

"In truth, people can generally make time for what they choose to do; it is not really the time, but the will that is lacking."

Sir John Lubbock

You've got to do it; for your own good. You won't be able to even look at your work if you don't take a day off and get a fresh perspective. If you're not looking at your work, then it's not getting done, so you might as well take the day off any way.

Is it making you ill? Time to see a counselor for professional help. Too expensive? Many workplaces have a service that allows for a few visits with a counselor to help you through your current problems. Your human resources department will also have some resources for you. Of course, you should talk with H.R. in private so your boss doesn't have to be involved in your personal or work-related problems.

Don't ignore your stress. Some stress is great for getting jobs done on time. But lots of stress is not healthy for you.

If you can, take a vacation. Take a week or two off if you can. It doesn't even have to be an expensive vacation to some exotic place. It can be in your own backyard, just so long as you get away from the job. Turn off your cell phone. Don't answer your home phone. Don't read work-related e-mails. Don't accept faxes. Don't get sucked back into your work during your vacation. Don't let them find you, even if you are just at home. Take the vacation time to do something you love to do. Or use it to work on your garden or some project that is not work related. Get outside. Breathe the fresh air. Go for a hike. Go to the mountains. Go to the beach, lake, or river. Just get out and do something different that helps you to forget about work. You will come back with a fresh perspective and be able to approach your tasks with renewed vigor.

If the vacation doesn't take the edge off, it might be time to look into other opportunities.

If you're the boss and your staff is trying to meet a deadline or they are going the extra mile to get the job done, it's time to treat them. It's time to show them that you are grateful for their hard work. Take them out for a department lunch. Make it a two-hour lunch so they don't have to hurry through the lunch. Order in a pizza. Pass out gift certificates to local restaurants. Highlight and praise the people in the group that are doing outstanding jobs. Many workers will go another extra mile for a few kind words and recognition in front of the staff. Whatever you do, it ought to be simple. There's no need to give raises, because that might become the expectation and you don't want to put yourself in a situation where you've raised their hopes for salary increases, especially in this up and down economy. Allow them to have a department party, where the food is potluck. This costs you nothing and increases goodwill. Even better; offer to pay for the main food, drinks, or nice dessert. It's all worth it. Happy co-workers are productive co-workers.

A word of caution about after hour parties, dinners or drinks: Many workers have families and would be unable to attend. Besides, going for drinks is not always a good idea because people behave differently after a few drinks and the possible surprises are endless. If you do go for drinks, you might offer to pay for taxi rides home for all concerned. Be responsible. After all, you could find yourself or your company liable if things go wrong. Drinks have the potential for a Human Resources' nightmare, so just be careful. In many companies, however, it is part of the culture. After-hour parties can be time spent with bosses and co-workers to learn more about them.

The point is that you give your team praise, recognition and most importantly, your attention. But also remember not to micromanage your team. Let them do the good work they're doing.

"The best executive is the one who has the sense enough to pick good men to do what he wants done, and self-restraint enough to keep from meddling with them while they do it."

Theodore Roosevelt

All of this is common sense. Get out there, get a job, and do the best you can. Work hard, take risks, respect people and move forward. Learn from your successes and failures. Don't let the failures bog you down. Remember Walt Disney and Milton Hershey. Their successes were not from smooth sailing. They both had seriously rough rides, but they worked through it, and succeeded despite all the bad weather. You can too.

Good luck!

CHAPTER 9

Common Sense & Timing at Home

"Your family and your love must be cultivated like a garden. Time, effort, and imagination must be summoned constantly to keep any relationship flourishing and growing.

Jim Rohn

"Acting is just a way of making a living; the family is life."

Denzel Washington

"Govern a family as you would cook a small fish — very gently."

Chinese Proverb

As you learn to be more aware of your common sense and use it to navigate through life as well as waiting for the right moment — timing — to take advantage of opportunities, you will also find that it's not all just about gaining financial and business success. All aspects of your life can be affected. Most importantly, common sense and timing with your family is a natural step. Using common sense and timing is a great way to lead your family through the bumps in life as well as to train your children to succeed in their own youthful ventures and adventures.

In this chapter, we'll discuss what we've learned in the preceding chapters and apply it to matters of the heart and home. A successful business is really only part of the battle in life. A successful family life is to many people the most important part of life. After all, many of us forget that the job is usually done so that we may create more opportunities for our family to live better, eat healthier, receive the best education, enable spectacular experiences like vacations and achieve comfortable shelter with all the toys and gadgets to make things interesting.

Common sense and timing will help you with your kids in various stages of their lives. Opportunities to guide them better, opportunities for understanding them, opportunities to teach them, and opportunities to help build confidence and wisdom as they trundle through life facing their own successes and failures. Give your kids the tools to do even better than you did.

Common sense and timing will also come in handy with your spouse. Guys, you can use timing much better with your wives — and you know it! Gals, common sense will help you understand your guys, especially when their timing is off — like when they've forgotten your anniversary again (Guys, common sense tells you that you ought to calendar important dates like her birthday and your wedding anniversary. Plan ahead — you will save yourself so much grief).

At many points in this chapter, you will probably

say to yourself, "Duh, I already do this, it's common sense." But even though you have good common sense, how many times do you still find yourself unprepared for the many things that you encounter during the day. How many times are you possibly setting a bad example for your kids? If you are doing everything and using your common sense, then kudos to you on your rare state of perfection—but do your kids have this same magic sense that you do? Or are you just really hoping that they do—projecting your sense of the world on them, when they have their own perceptions and unique personality? Sure, they're your kids, they're growing up and maybe following your role model, but for those of you who have two or more children, you know that each child is unique and quite unlike the other child or children in your home.

So, maybe common sense comes to you easily, but what about each of your kids? Heck, what about your spouse? Does he or she think the same way as you do? Odds are they don't. Each child, spouse, grandparent, aunt, uncle, cousin, etc. requires a different approach. Each is unique and you must see them for who they are. Never take them for granted. Lots of relatives do, but it's actually in defiance of common sense, and here's where the family problems multiply. Sometimes you can't actually see what's going on with the people closest to you—they're too close. It's hard to be objective. You must work harder to see each family member freshly every day.

FOCUS

Are you one of those parents who spends a lot of

time telling the kids what to do, when to do, how to do, do it this way, don't do it that way, do it the right way and, don't forget, do it now? Don't forget to take some time to focus on your child, or on each of your children. We as parents often get so wrapped up in our children not doing things the "right" way that we forget they are developing little human beings that also need to do things their way. If they try something and it doesn't work, they learn. You've got to remember to give them room to fail. How else are they going to learn to handle future "failures" in their adult lives? Let them try something their way. Focus on the things they are learning. Don't dwell on their mistakes. Focus on the things they are doing right. Praise them when they do something right. You don't have to be a psychologist to figure this out; it's common sense. You don't like it when your boss only focuses on what you're doing wrong. Why would your kids be any different?

Are you letting your children speak? When they speak, are you listening to them? Or are you thinking of all the things you've got to do later and tomorrow and the weekend? How are you going to set an example of a good listener if you're not even listening to them?

As we discussed earlier, listening is not just waiting for your turn to talk. It is not the time to prepare what you're going to say. It is the time to actually listen! Listen to what they say! Focus on your child who is trying to communicate with you. If you don't, they might give up trying to communicate with you. If you don't listen to them now, when they're older and not listening to you, then you won't have to wonder why they're not listening to you. You

183

already set the example.

Listen to them. Don't mock or make fun of them for saying something incorrectly or wrong. Just listen. Be sensitive to how you respond. Be respectful of them while they are talking—so that they will do the same when you are talking.

When you correct them, use constructive criticism. Kids don't understand all the subtle nuances of your response. They don't understand sarcasm. Speak clearly to them and positively. Be positive. If they are being negative, you might want to point out to them something positive that they haven't thought of. Don't assume that they will always know what you're talking about; even the older ones. It doesn't hurt to ask them if they have any questions.

And then listen to their comments.

If you don't listen, neither will they.

Treat your spouse the same way. Listen and don't assume halfway through the conversation what they're talking about.

Take the time to listen. There certainly won't be anytime later to make up for not listening, especially when you learn how fast your kids grow up. Listen to them now.

ORGANIZING AND ROUTINE-IZING

What was it about your childhood daily life that you liked or didn't like? Did your family have the same breakfast, lunch, and dinner routines every-day? Come hell or high water, hot food was on your plate, made by your mom or your dad.

Or was it every kid for himself? Breakfast, lunch and dinner only happened if you made it happen, and you only ate whatever was available in the fridge or the cupboards. Well, either way, you probably have an opinion about the style that works best for you now. You're either religious about your routines, or loose about them. What do you think your kids need?

I'd like to sell you on sticking to a specific routine. Kids don't need each day to be a mystery. They need stability. A consistently maintained routine provides a child the stability he or she needs to grow. They know what to expect each day, and they know what's expected of them.

Have you ever had a job where each day you came to work gritting your teeth because you just didn't know what you were supposed to do that day? Perhaps your boss just never took the time to explain to you what you were there for because to him or her it seemed obvious. That was probably one of the most frustrating jobs you ever had and you probably didn't stay there very long (or your boss didn't stay there very long). Kids don't really know what to expect unless you are consistent with them. Kids need a lot of explaining about many things—over and over. If you're expecting them to get all their learning from television, well, "Ozzie and Harriet" and "The Cosby Show" are no longer on the air anymore, are they? Imagine what they're watching nowadays and think of what they're learning. So, you will have to be the one to establish consistency in their lives. You will have to be the one to explain things to them so they're not gritting their teeth wondering what's going to happen today, tomorrow, and next year. Give them a road map to their life. You wouldn't go on a trip without a plan of where you're going. Let them know where they're going, where

185

the family's going.

If you're not a structured or organized person and you've got kids, you have got to provide for them a certain amount of structure and organization. Maybe you had too much structure and organization while you were growing up, so you're still rebelling against it. Maybe you never had any structure or organization. Whatever the case, there are plenty of books out there now that can help you to learn. Aren't your kids worth it?

"Bringing up a family should be an adventure, not an anxious discipline in which everybody is constantly graded for performance."

Milton R. Saperstein

A word of caution about organizing and establishing routines; there is a balance to everything and you do not need to go to the extreme where your kids feel like they're growing up in prison or in the military, where they start referring to you as "the dictator." Find that balance. Use your common sense. Of course, no matter what you do for your kids regarding structure and organization, they may still refer to you as "the dictator." Let's face it. To kids, being a parent often means being the "bad guy." But they'll thank you for it later.

STRESS MESS AND FAMILY

Are you under stress right now, because of your job, your marriage, or whatever? Are your kids under stress? Earlier, we covered the stress mess for you, but how can you take care of stress in the family situation. The same way as you would for yourself: put on the brakes!

If you, your spouse or your kids are under a lot of stress, stop what you or they are doing. Right away. Help them to escape the negativity they are feeling by helping them look for positive things.

Take a break by taking the family somewhere special, whether it's a weekend trip, or a day at the beach, a movie or a picnic in the park. Do it.

If it's your spouse who is stressing out, give him or her the day off. Take the kids out and let your spouse have a day of peace and quiet. Do it.

If it's you, have someone babysit the kids, or ask a relative to take the kids for a day. Do it.

If it's one of your kids, maybe it's time you took that child somewhere special. Maybe they feel like they're not getting enough attention. Maybe they feel they're getting too much attention (a teenager). Do something special with that child. Make sure you listen to them. Let them choose where they want to go or what they want to do. Let them know how important they are.

If it is a teenager and the stress that they are going through is not understandable to you, it might be a good time to consult a professional. Why not? They deal with teenagers all the time. Have you? Are you familiar with all the issues of a modern day teenager or are you just hiding your head in the sand just hoping they'll make it through without any serious troubles? Read up on what kids are going through these days. Consult people who know. Remember, what may have worked for you twenty years ago when you were in school, may no longer work now. After all, you probably never had to go through a metal detector to get to class.

If you are listening to your kids and your spouse, you will be more connected and know when it's time to put the brakes on.

Help them identify their problems. Get with your child or your spouse and ask them what's going on. Write down all the things they find stressful. That way, they can see the problems a little bit better. Once they are on paper they won't seem so overwhelming. Discuss possible solutions to these specific (or not so specific) problems with your child. Don't work it out for them though, let them try to figure it out themselves—they've got to learn these things themselves, but at least be there to listen and make suggestions. Don't rush in to solve their problems for them, give them time to figure it out on their own—you won't always be able to be there for them and this will allow them to learn how to solve their own problems.

You may have to ask your spouse if he or she wants to discuss possible solutions, but if you're the problem, you might want to get a professional to help. Your spouse may even feel better if you just sit down and listen to him or her vent. Just be sure to ask if they need help. If you don't ask, they may be too hurt to ask for your help and then you may find yourself in a bigger problem—when you least expect it!

Don't forget to prioritize the problems. Remember, some problems cannot be realistically solved. If the goldfish died, the feelings of your child may linger for quite some time. That's a different kind of stress for your child. (It may be time to explain your concept of heaven.) Your child won't be able to solve every problem, but each stress or problem is an opportunity for your child to learn something about how the world works. It's also an opportunity for you to be a caring parent.

Sometimes there is no way around stress for you, your spouse, or your child. The crying baby won't stop crying when you want it to and that difficult job situation won't go away until you find another. Sometimes you just have to suck it up and work though the stress. This is another important learning opportunity — often one of the hardest. What you can do is look for ways for the child to cope with these unavoidable stresses. Remember all children are born into this world with love. They know nothing else. We adults teach them how to hate. They learn from us. A happy child has less stress and feels better about themselves.

SELF-CONFIDENCE

Every parent wants his or her kids to get through each day on the strength of inner self-confidence. Well, if you're the parent that struggles with your own inner self-confidence, chances are pretty good that your kids are struggling too.

As we discovered earlier, self-confidence is a key to success, and we learned there is really no such thing as an overnight success. Success is something that's earned over time and through many trials. Self-confidence, if lacking, is something that needs to be practiced and built up over time and this can be done for kids too.

Kids can dress for success too. Remember, if you dress like you're a success, you will find that you feel like a success. Can this work for kids too? Yes! Of course, it doesn't mean that your kids have to keep up with the Joneses and honor every single fashion whim. Use your common sense. If they attend a private school with uniforms, make sure they wear the uniform properly and their shoes aren't scuffed and there aren't holes in the clothes. Iron their clothes, or teach them to iron their own clothes. Make sure the clothes get washed. You don't want your child to stand out because they look shabby. At many public schools, fashion seems to be anything goes, even the shabby look is in. But if your child lacks self-confidence, do you really think that's going to help them if they are wearing shabby clothes? You know their look influences how the teachers think of them. Try to figure out the balance line for your kids—from looking like their parents dressed them to what's fashionable. Have your kids' hair cut. Get them braces if they need them. Make sure they bathe everyday. Make sure they brush their teeth everyday. It's up to you to instill these habits in them. These are the basic habits that can make them feel better about themselves.

If your child is overweight, you should work with your doctor or a professional so that you can take steps to help your child. This can have an incredible impact on their self-confidence.

As we learned, self-confidence comes from being prepared. This doesn't mean your child has to join the Boy or Girl Scouts to "be prepared" (but don't knock the Scouts as it is an excellent organization for teaching your children to improve themselves). It means not "winging it". Your child needs to learn to study for tests and prepare for speeches. If ever you have a business presentation to give, let your child watch you prepare for it. If your child has a report to do, depending upon the child's age, show him or her how to get ready for a report. If you don't know how, call someone who does know. Parents, you should never use the excuse "I don't know how to do that" or "They never taught me that when I was your age" with your child. You know how to find things out. If you know how to ask a friend a question, then you can certainly find out all sorts of things. Don't give your child that excuse—because they'll use it later on too. Ask the questions. I'm not saying give your child the answers. I'm saying if you don't know how to find information, ask someone who does—a librarian, a teacher, a relative, or jump online. There are so many resources nowadays.

Teaching your child how to prepare things for himself or herself will give that child a boost in self-confidence. Have your child prepare his or her lunch the night before school. Have your child lay out his or her clothes the night before. Have your child plan their own weekend activities.

Teach them to think about things they're going to need. Teach them to think ahead. This takes us back to giving your child a roadmap, so he or she knows where they're heading.

Prepare your child to learn how to prepare—it's priceless information and all part of their growing self-confidence.

Teach them how to overcome bad habits and to soften their harder personality habits. Teach them to be positive. Build that fire within them to believe in themselves.

If you don't have it yourself, you better start building that fire within yourself. Your child is watching you. What do you want him or her to learn from you? If you're negative, your child could become negative. Don't you want to break that habit?

Finally, when it comes to self-confidence, it comes easily when you're doing what you love. The same thing happens with kids too. If you see that your child naturally gravitates to something, build that up, encourage it. If your child is athletic and loves to play sports, get him or her involved in sports. If your child is more academic, encourage and support that too. Visit more museums or enroll him or her in advanced classes. Pay for piano lessons or whatever instrument they're interested in.

When the sports, academic, or music opportunities become harder and they want to quit — don't let them quit! Teach them to work through the hard times. Teach them to stretch further to do better. (Please note, if it's apparent that they are no longer interested in the subject or activity, it may truly be time to end that subject or activity. Listen to your child and as always, use your common sense.)

Sports and any other interests like hobbies, academics and music, can be such a gift to your child. The return on the investment is priceless. Any of these interests can be the perfect laboratory for growing self-confidence in your child.

Again, this all may seem like common sense, but how many people do you know take the time to take these steps? Maybe they do at their workplace, but what about at home?

IMAGINATION PLUS

When you first get married, you have goals that you work on together, then the kids come along and your goals often change. Often the goals become lost altogether. You, your spouse, and your family forget to dream big, or put the big dreams on hold until that magical day when you have all the time in the world to focus on your dreams — that day when the kids are all grown up or that day when you retire. Do you really want to wait that long? That magical day — that impossible and unrealistic day — is probably when you're lying on your deathbed and you've only got a few minutes left to think of all the things you should have done or wanted to do. I really don't suggest waiting for the perfect time when you can focus on the things you wanted to do. Life speeds by way too fast.

So break out that imagination of yours and get your family involved. Dream big! Find out what your family's dreaming about. Find out what your spouse is dreaming about. Tell them about your dreams.

Make sure you get everyone to the dinner table regularly to talk about these things. Plan a dinner-time once a week, where each person gets a chance to talk about his or her dreams. Set some rules so that negativity and sarcasm aren't allowed at the dinner table.

I think in the last few decades, the power and magic of dinnertime discussions have been lost to the fast-paced world with dinner in front of the television or at a noisy fast food restaurant.

Use your family's imagination to problem solve.

Use them to dream about vacations they want to take. Use them to dream about careers. Imagine how your children would feel if they were included on solving problems? Perhaps they're at an age where it wouldn't make much sense to them, but once old enough, they'll be familiar with the process and take to it easily. Can you imagine?

If you can't at least imagine possibilities, there is too much dust on your imagination and you need to shake things up and break out the imagination again! You've stopped growing. If you've stopped growing, how is your family going to learn to grow and improve?

As we discussed earlier, you've got to think about the things that are holding you back. Are you still thinking the same way you did twenty years ago? How about your kids?

Are your kids afraid to do some things, to get involved, to pursue something that has an element of risk? How are you going to break them of that pattern? How are they ever going to learn that they can actually try and if they try, sometimes they're going to get past the obstacles and break through? That's what life's all about. You need to encourage your children to stretch, to try, and even fail sometimes. Failure's all right. It will be worth it when they get that first success; when they learn not to give up. Once they prove to themselves that they're capable of doing and succeeding at challenging things, now you've got a child who is on the road to achievement.

Get your children to imagine, dream and try. If you've forgotten how, or you never tried, it's time to start figuring it out. It's time to take chances. What do you have to lose? If not for yourself, do it for your kids.

If your child or teenager is dreaming of being a baseball player, an Olympic gymnast, an actor, a fireman, or whatever, encourage the dream. Sign them up for Little League or gymnastics. Send them to a beginning class on acting. Visit a fire station. Can't afford sign-ups? No classes available? Go to the library and read up on these things. Find age appropriate books on the subject of their interest and read it with them. Check out videos on the subjects. Go on line and read up about it. Do something! And don't dampen their spirits! If it's something you don't want them doing, just remember, once they're exposed to it or learn more about it, they may indeed lose their interest. They'll change their minds often so don't discourage them. Let them make the decision themselves without your interference. What do you think they'll do if you interfere? They'll probably focus on it even more just to get a rise out of you. However, if they do get discouraged, talk to them or work with them to discover other new activities and things to do. Help to get them over their discouragement.

If your child wants to go to college, and you never went to college yourself, find out what to do to get your child on that road. Start them on that road early. Don't wait until their senior year in high school — that's too late. Encourage them to keep their grades up to meet their goal. Make sure they get into the right college preparatory classes. Talk to their counselors and their teachers. Find out how your child is doing in class from first grade all the way through high school. Stay on top of everyone. Don't let them blow you off. Don't settle for second best, and don't settle for partial answers to your questions. Your child's future depends upon it. Dream big for your child's future and work hard so that it happens.

Dream up things for your family to do together. Have your kids dream up a family vacation. Go do something together.

You don't have to spend any money to do something together. Play a board game together. Have a picnic at the park. Go to the beach. Have a movie or DVD day and catch up on a movie together. Go to a museum. The city you live in probably has a magazine or newspaper that lists family events. Pick one up and bring it to the dinner table and go over the available activities. Decide on when and DO IT!!!

Is work getting in the way of your family dream? Sometimes it will, and that's okay; it's part of the responsibility of earning enough money to keep your family fed and sheltered. But if you haven't seen your kids in a few days or weeks, then it may be time for you to focus on your family. After all, someone once said that no one ever wishes on their deathbed that they had worked more.

LIFE ISSUES

Take the time to talk to your kids about life issues, like religion, sex, drugs, smoking, death, morality, how to treat others, etc. If you don't talk to them about these issues, their school will. Or they'll learn it from TV, or yikes, MTV. Or worse, they will learn everything from their friends.

Discuss with your children what your beliefs are.

Talk to them about the God of your religion; what the belief in the afterlife is. Talk about the rules of your religion. Make sure they attend classes or Sunday school, if offered. Discuss how they should treat people who have different beliefs.

If you want your kids to behave a certain way, you are really the best role model for them—you're the first adult they see on a day to day basis. So, set a good example. Be responsible. Be honest. Don't pretend to be responsible and honest—your kids are watching you... always, and it sinks in when they catch you being otherwise.

If you're calling in "sick" to work just to get a day off, don't be surprised if your child wants to call in "sick" to school.

If you cut corners and take a lot of "shortcuts" (for example, you just quickly want to park and you go for the nearest handicapped spot), don't be surprised if your newly licensed teenager does the same thing.

If you speed, they will too.

If you give the finger to someone who cuts you off, they will too.

There are often more dangerous consequences to these bad habits. Do you really want your child to face worse consequences just because he or she mimics your bad habits? It could happen. Why chance it.

White lies oftentimes indicate to your child that telling a lie is okay. If you talk about your mother-in-law behind her back, don't be surprised if your child repeats it in front of her.

Cheat a little bit here and a little bit there, then maybe it's okay for your child to cheat on a test and later cheat on their taxes, or worse. These are habits you never want to instill in your child. It is weak and will bring about your downfall or your child's downfall.

Again, this is all common sense, but how many times do we have to think about these things after the damage has been done?

I'm not saying you have to be perfect, but, from time to time, just do a personal checkup. Everyone should stop and think about how they're raising their kids, treating their spouse, treating their fellow man or woman.

Think about the goals you're chasing after. Just stop and think about them. We get so busy these days our minds are on autopilot and time's flying by faster and faster.

Love and listen to your family. Guide them and grow!

CHAPTER 10
Mind Drills

Now lets do a little mind drill and focus on what life is really like... Read each of my life's tidbits. After you have read them, I want you to think and analyze their meaning. Copy the one you like, hang it up and read it.

- How do you know what you can do until you do it?

- Everyone can be a working manager...but not everyone can be a leader.

- How do you know if you can do it, if you haven't tried to do it.

- There are people that talk about doing it, but never do it at all, and then there is a person that just does it.

- Success is like SURVIVAL; you want it or you don't. The choice is yours.

- Life doesn't always turn out the way you

plan it, so when an opportunity comes up, take it.

- There is no point in learning something unless you apply it... then you should take your knowledge and turn it into a skill.

- To make a change, you must plan.

- Everyone gets at least one chance in life to do something great... then after you accomplish your greatness you will get another chance.

- There are leaders, managers, supervisors, followers and workers... Do you know the difference? Leaders are born.

- Everyone in the world has one thing in common... The little dash between the day they were born and the day they die. That little dash represents what they accomplished in their life. There is no getting away from that dash so why not go for your dreams and goals.

- If you can dream it.... you can do it.

- Be kind... be nice to everyone you talk to. You never know if they might be president some day.

- In order to win and accomplish your goals in life, you must have desire.

- There is always hope and if you have

hope, you have a chance to make things happen. The rest is up to you.

- Nobody is going to make you successful. You must take the first step and apply your talents. Once you apply your talents, then the people around you will make you more successful.

- Dreams are made by people who see the future... successful people are always dreaming.

- Nobody appreciates anything until they don't have it anymore.

- Never worry about failing because then you will end up worrying about it because you haven't tried to do it, or you just talked about it and then you might have missed your chance. There are doers and talkers. Talkers never win.

- Life has many challenges and when you fall down, it doesn't matter how far you fall. It's much faster to bounce back up and recover.

- Do you know the meaning of RISK? To keep winning you have to lose a little.

- If you have to ask how much... you can't afford it in the first place.

- No matter how rich or poor you are, you are always faced with the same risk factor, the difference is the recovery factor.

- You have only one time to make a first impression. So why not go for the gold first time around, you might not get another chance.

- It's not how you do things, it's what we do that matters.

- It's much easier to make money if you are a rich person, so why not think rich.

- Remember, everything starts out as an idea.

- Progress comes one day at a time.

- Don't be afraid of change... it only happens as fast as you want it to.

- Anything is possible when you dream. Anything can be impossible if you don't try.

- Anyone who says they never makes mistakes, is a person who never tries.

- Everyday should be a positive day for you. Life is based on three elements - 0 +. Always get rid of the - (negative) and everything will become a + (positive).

- Experiencing success is great... but having someone know about your success and appreciate it is the real success.

- The trick in life is to get smart at a young

age so as you get older you can use your knowledge.

- Always remember your failure can be your greatest success.

- Memories only come in one-shot, and you never know when the shot is coming until it has passed. Then you're only left with the memory, so make every shot count in business and in life.

- It is crucial to recognize that awareness is the first step to any solution.

- Everyone in life will be faced with pitfalls. One of the best ways to avoid them is to associate yourself with successful people. People make people successful.

- The way to be nothing is to do nothing.

- Negative thoughts produce negative reactions.

- One of the facts in life that everyone shares is that there are no limits on the income everyone makes. It's up to you on the limit you are happy with. Knowledge works the same way.

- The harder it comes closer to success, the harder it is to succeed. If it was so easy then everyone would be doing it.

- A smart person will plan his work and then work his plan.

- Every successful person has a growth pattern. Awareness is the first step to solve a solution. Everyone has pitfalls and will face obstacles in life. Successful people try to avoid them.

- If there is a race for success there would be no finish line.

- You can never learn anything if you keep talking; listening is your key to knowledge. Knowledge is something you never have enough of.

- Life is a designation from the time you're born until you die. So enjoy the trip and make the most of the ride.

- The only competition you have in life is the time to accomplish your own goals.

I am going to end "Common Sense and Timing" with something that I hope you will always remember...

"The greatness of a person is not in their wealth or knowledge they have. It's judged in the value and ability on the way they touch someone's life."

Michael J. Cutino